the

Inter

Dictionary
of
Personal Finance

Beneficiary *A.T.M*

Nominal Yield

chartist bargain

Nasdaq **capital assets**

Amortization

Call Option **actuals**

Bull Market

⌐⌐⌐ TTL

TTL is an imprint of
Take That Ltd.
P.O.Box 200
Harrogate
HG1 2YR
ENGLAND

email:sales@takethat.co.uk
Fax: +44-1423-526035

**For more financial and investment books from TTL, visit
http://www.takethat.co.uk/Fbooks.htm**

You should take independent financial advice before acting on material contained in this book.

TTL are always keen to receive ideas and manuscripts for new
financial books. Please send details to the address above.

ISBN 1-873668-54-6

Preface

This book is intended to assist those who are either interested personally, or involved by way of their work, in personal finance. It has been prepared to give short, precise, easy to understand definitions of the more commonly used terms and jargon in the USA and the UK.

You are sure to find it useful when reading the financial pages of the national press, money magazines and company reports, and when dealing with your financial adviser and/or broker.

Whilst there are many terms sharing the same definitions on both sides of the Atlantic, there are also others with very different meanings, which are defined accordingly. Subject areas covered by the definitions include those of annuities, banks and banking, bonds, business, equities (shares, mutual funds/unit trusts, investment trusts), insurance, pensions, taxation and wills.

Please note that words and phrases which appear as SMALL CAPITALS are cross-referenced elsewhere in the dictionary.

AJ Rider

Also in the same series:
The International Dictionary of Derivatives
For a brochure of financial market and personal investment titles from TTL, please write to TTL, PO Box 200, Harrogate HG1 2YR, England

A

abandonment [USA]   The voluntary relinquishing of all rights, title or possession of property such as trademarks, copyrights and patents etc. **[UK]** A situation where an OPTION HOLDER allows ownership of an option to expire unexercised.

acceptance   The writing of the word 'accepted' on the face of a BILL OF EXCHANGE by the drawee together with his/her signature indicating acceptance to pay the bill when due.

accepting house [UK]   An organisation, usually a MERCHANT BANK, which accepts or guarantees BILLS OF EXCHANGE.

Access   A former CREDIT CARD system which was sold to MASTERCARD and discontinued.

accident insurance   INSURANCE which pays benefits in the event of an accident. Items typically covered are medical expenses and loss of earnings. If, for example, the insured sustains the loss of a limb or an eye, a specified lump sum is payable.

accidental death insurance   INSURANCE which pays a lump sum in the event of death of the insured being caused by an accident.

account   A facility, provided by financial institutions such as banks, in which an individual can keep money.

account balance [USA]   The net credit or debit balance of an ACCOUNT at the end of a reporting period.

account payee [UK]   Also 'account payee only.' Words written on the face of a cheque between two parallel diagonal lines. The purpose is to ensure that the cheque may only be paid into an account in the name of the payee, that is the person to whom the cheque is made payable. This means that the payee cannot sign it in favour of another person.

accounts payable   Amounts owed *by* an organisation or individual to another for goods or services it has received.

accounts receivable   Amounts *due* to an organisation or individual from another for goods or services it has supplied.

accrual   A term used in company accounts where income is due or a cost is incurred during an accounting period but has not been received or paid.

accrued benefits   Benefits earned by an employee in respect of his/her pension based on years of service with his/her employer.

accumulated dividend   A dividend due to holders of CUMULATIVE PREFERRED STOCK (USA) or CUMULATIVE PREFERENCE SHARES (UK) but not yet paid. The amount is carried forward on the books as a liability until paid.

accumulation [USA]   Regular investment in a MUTUAL FUND with dividends reinvested.

accumulation units [UK]   Units in a UNIT TRUST where dividends, less basic rate tax, paid by companies in which the trust invests, are reinvested to increase the fund's unit value.

acid test   See liquidity ratio.

acquisition   A term used to describe the takeover of a company by another.

Act of God   An unpreventable and unpredictable event which could cause loss or damage to buildings, land, vehicles etc. Acts of God can be insurable.

actuals   Commodities such as metals, coffee and grain which are bought and sold for use as opposed to HEDGING by trading on a FUTURES CONTRACT.

actuary   A person trained and specialising in risk, statistics and finance and as such gives advice on insurance and pension business. Calculations made by actuaries include such items as premiums, bonus payments and life expectancy etc.

additional pension [UK]   See SERPS.

additional personal allowance [UK]   An income tax allowance to single persons including widows/widowers, separated spouses etc who are not entitled to married couple's allowance and are supporting a child under the age of 16 at their own expense. This allowance also applies where a man's wife is living with him and she is totally incapacitated and they have a child living with them.

additional rate tax [UK] A term which applies to trusts without an interest in possession (for example a discretion-ary trust) and defines the additional rate of tax on income.

additional voluntary contributions (AVC) Additional payments to a TAX DEFERRED savings account or an OCCUPATIONAL PENSION SCHEME by an employee to boost a pension at retirement.

adjustable rate mortgage (ARM) [USA] A MORTGAGE where the interest rate is liable to change over the term of the loan and which is dependent on influences such as interest rates on US TREASURY SECURITIES.

adjustable rate preferred stock (ARPS) [USA] PREFERRED STOCK which pays a dividend in line with interest rates generally rather than a fixed dividend.

adjusted gross income [USA] A person's income on which federal income tax is calculated. This is GROSS INCOME less adjustments such as Individual Retirement Account, Simplified Employee Pension Plan, Keogh Plan and alimony payments but before itemized deductions such as state and local income taxes, interest expenses and medical expenses.

administrator (feminine form administratrix) An individual legally appointed by a court to settle the affairs of a deceased person who failed to make a will. An administrator is also appointed in cases where the deceased person made a will but failed to name an EXECUTOR or the executor predeceased or fails to act for some other reason.

advisory account [UK] An individual's account with a stockbroker where both advice is given and dealing conducted if required.

affidavit A written statement signed on oath and witnessed by an authorised person such as a notary public (USA) or a commissioner for oaths, invariably a solicitor (UK).

after hours deals Dealings made on a stock exchange after its official closure time. These deals are rolled over and included in the following day's transactions.

age admitted [UK] A term used on occasions in LIFE ASSURANCE policy documents, which indicates that the ASSURED has proven his/her age by giving sight of his/her birth certificate to the insurance company. This means that no further evidence of age will be needed in the event of a subsequent claim that is the death of the assured or maturity of the policy.

age allowance [UK]   An additional personal allowance and additional married couple's allowance for persons aged 65 to 74 regarding income tax. A further increase in age allowance is applicable for persons aged 75 and over.

agency   A business operated by an AGENT in conjunction with his/her PRINCIPAL.

agency securities [USA]   Securities issued by federal government agencies.

agent   A person appointed by a PRINCIPAL to act on the latter's behalf in business.

aggressive growth fund [USA]   A MUTUAL FUND which invests in the stocks of rapid growth companies. Such companies pay little or no dividends, the prime purpose of this type of fund being to achieve greater than average capital appreciation. However the investment risk is correspondingly greater. Also known as maximum capital gains fund or capital appreciation fund.

alimony   Money paid to a divorced or separated spouse according to a divorce order.

allocation notice (assignment form/notice)   A formal notification to the WRITER of an OPTION from a clearing house (corporation) that an option has been exercised by an option HOLDER and that the writer is obliged to buy/sell the UNDERLYING INSTRUMENT at the EXERCISE PRICE to meet his/her obligations.

allotment   The distribution of shares to applicants. This may be for the full amount or, if OVERSUBSCRIBED, a proportion of the full amount.

allotment notice/letter   A confirming document from the company concerned that newly issued shares have been allotted to the applicant.

allowances [UK]   Amounts which may be deducted from a person's GROSS INCOME prior to calculation of income tax. For example PERSONAL ALLOWANCE. See deduction [UK].

allowable expenses   Expenses incurred by a person whilst carrying out duties at work, which are 'approved' by the tax authorities and can be offset against income to reduce taxable pay.

alpha shares [UK]   A term previously given to the most actively traded shares on the LONDON STOCK EXCHANGE along with beta, gamma and delta shares. This classification was replaced by the NORMAL MARKET SIZE classification in January 1991.

Alternative Investment Market (AIM) [UK]   A market for small, young and growing companies operated by the LONDON STOCK EXCHANGE as a regulated market of a RECOGNISED INVESTMENT EXCHANGE and set up in June 1995.   It effectively replaced the UNLISTED SECURITIES MARKET (USM).   The market provides an opportunity for companies to raise capital for expansion, a trading facility and a way of establishing a market value for their shares.

alternative minimum tax (AMT) [USA]   A tax which targets high wealth individuals to pay a minimum amount of tax. The tax is calculated on the sum of adjusted gross income and tax preference items less exemptions.

American Association of Individual Investors   An association located in Chicago whose purpose is to provide information and education regarding stocks, mutual funds and bonds etc to individual investors.

American depositary receipt (ADR) [USA]   A receipt for the shares of a foreign company.   The share certificate is issued and held by an American bank.

American Express   An international company whose services include travel and financial products and which is probably most well known for the American Express CHARGE CARD which enables the holder to obtain goods and services without the need to pay cash.   Invoices of transactions are tendered monthly which must be settled in full.   There is no preset spending limit.

American Stock Exchange (AMEX)   A stock exchange located in Manhattan where stocks of small to medium sized companies are traded.

American style option   An OPTION which may be exercised by the holder into its UNDERLYING INSTRUMENT at any time until expiry.   See also European style option.

amortisation   The reducing of the value of an asset to zero over a period of time.

analyst   A person who analyses data relevant to a subject such as securities in order to make recommendations.

angel [USA] 1. An INVESTMENT GRADE bond. **2.** A provider of VENTURE CAPITAL. **[UK]** A provider of capital for theatrical productions.

annual meeting [USA] annual general meeting (AGM) [UK] An annual meeting, called by the directors of a company, which shareholders are invited to attend. Subjects normally discussed include audited accounts, election or re-election of directors and dividend payments to shareholders.

annual percentage rate (APR) Where interest on loans is expressed as other than a yearly rate, for example 1.5% per month, APR is the equivalent rate over a year, in this case 19.56%*. This enables would be borrowers to compare rates and to see the true extent of the rate of interest repayment they would incur.

* *To calculate APR*

$$r = 100 [(1 + i/100) - 1]$$

where r = effective annual rate (APR) as a percentage   i = the period rate
(for example 1.5 % in the example above)
m = number of periods in a year   (for example 12 for a monthly rate)

annual report A statement of a corporation's or company's performance over a year together with the accounts which is sent to shareholders.

annual return [USA] The total annual return on an investment which includes dividend payments and capital gains/losses. Not included are transactions costs and taxes. **[UK] 1.** Another term for a person's yearly TAX RETURN. **2.** An obligatory return, submitted annually to the REGISTRAR OF COMPANIES, detailing information regarding a company's operations including business description, details of directors and company secretary, share capital etc.

annuitant A person in receipt of an ANNUITY.

annuitize [USA] The commencement of regular payments from capital which has accumulated in an ANNUITY.

annuity [USA] A type of contract in which an individual (the annuitant) builds up capital (tax deferred) in a savings account with a life insurance company, usually for retirement income. At retirement, the annuitant then begins drawing an income (known as annuitizing) which is subject to tax. There are two main types, *fixed annuity* and *variable annuity*. A *fixed annuity* guarantees payments which are fixed for life or a specific period. With a *variable annuity* payments to the annuitant vary and will depend on the performance of the insurance company's underlying investments.

annuity [UK] The payment of a regular income from a life company to an annuitant in exchange for a lump sum either for life or shorter periods. Annuities are typically used for pensions and the individual receiving the annuity is known as an annuitant. In the UK they can broadly be classified into two types, *compulsory purchase annuity* and *purchased life annuity*. A *compulsory purchase annuity* is bought from the proceeds of a PENSION fund and is taxable as earned income. A *purchased life annuity* is bought with an individual's own capital and is taxed at a lower rate than a compulsory purchase annuity. There are three different types of pension annuities commonly referred to as standard annuities, with profits annuities and unit linked annuities. Standard pension annuities are the most commonly purchased and account for over ninety percent of the UK market. The income from a standard pension annuity is guaranteed for the rest of the annuitant's life whereas the income from a with profits or unit linked annuity will fluctuate depending on the investment performance of the underlying assets. There are various options which can be provided including, *annuity certain:* Income is paid for a given period whether or not death of the individual occurs. *deferred annuity:* Income which does not commence until some future specified date. *escalating annuity:* Income which increases annually by a given amount, for example 3%. The choosing of this option results in lower income compared with a level annuity over the initial years. *immediate annuity:* An annuity which starts to pay income soon after it has come into operation, for example at the end of the month following the payment of the lump sum. *joint life annuity:* Income usually relevant to two persons (for example man and wife) which continues until the death of the first person only. *joint life and survivor annuity:* Income usually relevant to two persons (for example man and wife) which continues until the death of the second person. *level annuity:* Income which is paid at a fixed rate throughout the life of the individual. See also guaranteed minimum period. *temporary annuity:* Income is paid either for a fixed period or until earlier death.

annuity certain See annuity.

annuity starting date The date on which annuity benefit payments commence to an annuitant.

appropriate personal pension plan [UK] A pension plan in which employer and employee pay full rate NATIONAL INSURANCE contributions equivalent to the employee contracting into SERPS. This rate will clearly be greater than the rate paid by contracting out of SERPS. The difference between these rates, the contracted-out rebate, is paid by the Department of Social Security (DSS) into a scheme known as an appropriate personal pension plan which buys pension benefits at retirement age known as PROTECTED RIGHTS. Provided an employee qualifies, incentive payments may also be paid by the DSS into the scheme. The contracted-out rebate plus any incentive payments are known as minimum contributions. Payment of minimum contributions into an appropriate personal pension plan results in a reduction of SERPS benefit at retirement age as though the employee had contracted out through a FINAL SALARY related scheme.

approved investment trust [UK]   An INVESTMENT TRUST which satisfies certain conditions set by the tax authorities and accordingly is exempt from tax on capital gains made on profits from sales of investments within its portfolio.

approved list [USA]   A list of investments in which a financial institution such as a MUTUAL FUND is authorised to invest.

arbitrage   The exploitation of price differentials between one market and another by simultaneously purchasing in one and selling in the other, such items as COMMODITIES, exchange rates, stocks etc.

arbitrageur   A person or firm carrying out ARBITRAGE.

arrearage [USA]   The amount of interest due on bonds and dividends due on CUMULATIVE PREFERRED STOCK but as yet unpaid. Whilst dividends on cumulative preferred stock remain unpaid, dividends on COMMON STOCK are not payable.

articles of association [UK]   The document which lists the regulations that govern the running of a company which include shareholder's voting rights, directors duties and general working and management etc. They are registered with the MEMORANDUM OF ASSOCIATION when the company is formed

articles of incorporation [USA]   The document which the founders of a corporation submit to the relevant state for approval after which a certificate of incorporation is issued. These two documents form the corporation's charter which endorses its legality. Information listed in the charter includes the name of the corporation, purpose, number of authorised shares and details of directors. The rules under which the corporation's internal management operates are listed in the BYLAWS.

ask price   The price at which a seller will trade a security or commodity. Also known as offer price.

assay   The testing of a metal to determine its degree of purity or to establish the constituents of an alloy (a mixture of metals).

asset allocation   The proportion of money allocated to various investments such as bonds, stocks, real estate and cash etc.

assets   Possessions owned by individuals or businesses having a monetary value. A corporation's assets can be referred to as tangible and intangible. Tangible assets include debtors, cash, stock and machinery etc. Intangible assets are those which cannot be seen and include such items as goodwill and patents etc.

assignee   A person to whom an asset or right is assigned.

assignment (assign)   The transfer of ownership of an item from one person to another.

assignment form/notice   See allocation notice.

assignor   A person who assigns an asset or right to another party.

Association of Investment Trust Companies (AITC) [UK]
An association formed in 1932 to represent the interests of INVESTMENT TRUST companies. Its main aims are the protection and promotion of the interests of its members and their shareholders.

Association of Private Client Investment Managers and Stockbrokers (APCIMS) [UK]   An association formed in 1990 to represent the interests of stockbroking and investment management firms which specialise in the provision of services for private investors (Also known as private clients). Member stockbrokers are members of the LONDON STOCK EXCHANGE and regulated in the main by the SECURITIES AND FUTURES AUTHORITY (SFA). Investment management firms are regulated by the INVESTMENT MANAGEMENT REGULATORY ORGANISATION (IMRO)

Association of Unit Trusts and Investment Funds (AUTIF) [UK]
A trade association formed in 1959 to represent the interests of its members and known then as the Unit Trust Association. The Association was renamed AUTIF in April 1993. Its main objectives are improving the regulatory environment, increasing public awareness and providing information and assistance to its members.

assurance [UK]   In the UK the term 'assurance' tends to be used where INSURANCE is taken out against something which will inevitably occur, an example being death and thus LIFE ASSURANCE. The term 'insurance' is used when insuring against an event which *may* occur such as damage to a motor vehicle. See ENDOWMENT ASSURANCE. See insurance.

assured   In the UK the assured is a person (or persons) who has entered into a LIFE ASSURANCE contract with a life office and is the policyholder. The person on whose life the policy is taken out is known as the LIFE ASSURED. The assured and the life assured are often the same person but not always. In the USA the expression 'insured' is used. In life insurance, the insured is the person (or persons) who has entered into a contract and on whose life the policy is written. On the death of the insured the face amount of the policy passes to the beneficiary.

ATM card   A plastic card enabling the holder to access an automated teller machine to obtain cash and statements.

at the money   A situation where the EXERCISE PRICE of a call/put option approximates to the current market price of the UNDERLYING INSTRUMENT.

audit   The official examination of a company's accounts by a qualified accountant external to the company.

auditor   A person appointed by a company to perform an audit.

authorised share capital [UK]   The total amount of capital (money) a company is authorised to raise by reference to its articles and memorandum of association.

authorized stock [USA]   The total number of shares which a corporation may issue by reference to its ARTICLES OF INCORPORATION.

authorised unit trust [UK]   A UNIT TRUST which has applied for and received approval from the FINANCIAL SERVICES AUTHORITY (FSA) as being suitable for promotion in the UK. Such unit trusts are exempt from CAPITAL GAINS TAX within the trust.

automated pit trading   A computer based trading system operating in FUTURES markets incorporating the features of OPEN OUTCRY transactions.

automated teller machine (ATM)   Also known as cash dispenser. A computerised self service machine allowing the holder of an ATM card and authorised personal identification number (PIN) to obtain cash and statements etc.

automobile insurance [USA]   INSURANCE taken out by the INSURED for cover against automobile damage or loss such as collision or theft and for cover against injuries to persons, damage to property and medical expenses. In the UK this is known as motor insurance.

averaging   A term used to describe additional purchases of shares in a company or companies when the price has fallen which has the effect of lowering the average buying price.

B

back end load [USA]   A charge imposed when redeeming shares in MUTUAL FUNDS to discourage withdrawals. These charges often reduce to zero over a period of time, typically five years. Also known as deferred sales charge. In the UK this is known as an exit charge.

back taxes [USA]   Taxes that have not been paid on the due date or were underreported either by accident or by intention on a past tax return. The tax authorities can demand payment of back taxes plus the imposing of penalties.

back to back loan [UK]   A situation where an investment organisation, such as an INVESTMENT TRUST, deposits sterling with a UK bank which subsequently arranges with a foreign associate bank to lend the equivalent amount of foreign currency to the investment organisation. The purpose of this transaction is to HEDGE against currency fluctuations affecting the portfolio.

back to back plan [UK]   The combination of a LIFE ASSURANCE policy and an ANNUITY on the same life with the purpose of reducing INHERITANCE TAX. The ANNUITANT seeks to replace capital expended for the annuity by paying premiums on a life policy, the proceeds of which pass to his/her dependants on death and outside the estate.

backwardation   A FUTURES market term where the nearby price of a COMMODITY exceeds the FORWARD PRICE.

BACS Limited [UK]   BACS Limited is an APACS clearing company which provides an automated clearing service for payments originated by SETTLEMENT MEMBERS or those they sponsor.

balanced mutual fund [USA]   A MUTUAL FUND which invests in a balance of COMMON STOCK, BONDS and PREFERRED STOCK with an objective of income provision and some capital appreciation with low risk.

balance of payments (BOP)   A country's financial position, with other countries of the world, which is made up of its current account and capital account (or capital movement) over a given period of time. The current account covers the balance of imports and exports. (See balance

---

of trade). The capital account covers the difference between capital invested in other countries and by other countries.

balance of trade (BOT)   The difference between exports and imports of visible (for example, manufactured goods) and invisible (for example, insurance) items over a given period of time.

balance sheet   A statement showing the ASSETS, LIABILITIES and CAPITAL of a company enabling its financial status to be observed at a particular time.

Baltic Exchange   A self regulated London exchange serving world wide interests. It is the world's premier maritime market for ship chartering and sale and purchase. The Exchange publishes a range of market information and freight derivatives price settlements.

balloon [USA]   The final payment on a loan which is significantly larger than those preceding it.

band earnings [UK]   Pay between the LOWER EARNINGS LIMIT and UPPER EARNINGS LIMIT which is used to determine NATIONAL INSURANCE CONTRIBUTIONS.

bank   An institution organised to receiving money from individuals, corporations, organisations etc. and making payments on their behalf and to make profit for itself. It may arrange loans for both individuals and companies and charges interest during the repayment period. Money deposited with a bank may also itself earn interest. In the USA, banks are regulated under the FEDERAL RESERVE SYSTEM. Banks operating in the UK, formerly regulated by the Bank of England, are now authorised and supervised by the FINANCIAL SERVICES AUTHORITY.

bank credit [USA]   The maximum credit an individual may secure from his/her bank.

bank giro credit [UK]   A system operated by the clearing banks in which a paper slip/document instructs a bank branch to credit a sum of money to a specified account at that branch.

bank insurance fund [USA]   A fund held by a section of the FEDERAL DEPOSIT INSURANCE CORPORATION as deposit insurance for banks excluding THRIFTS.

bank line [USA]   A moral, rather than a contractual commitment by a bank to provide a loan to a borrower up to a stated total amount over a stated period, typically one year. Because a bank line is not a legal commitment, it is not usual to for a commitment fee to be charged. However it is often necessary to keep compensating balances on deposit, typically 10% of the bank line plus an additional 10% of actual borrowings. Where customers are officially notified in respect of a line the term is advised line or confirmed line. In cases where the bank sets an internal guide and the customer is not notified the term is guidance line. Bank line is also known as a line of credit.

Bank of England   The central bank of the United Kingdom working in conjunction with the government as its banker and maintaining the integrity and value of the nation's currency. It ensures the stability and promotes the efficiency and competitiveness of the financial system and has operational responsibility for setting interest rates in order to achieve the government's inflation target. The Bank also manages the government's foreign currency borrowing programme, is responsible for market intervention in support of the government's exchange rate policy and controls the design, production and issue of banknotes in England and Wales. It is currently involved in practical preparations for European and Monetary Union to ensure the UK remains competitive whether or not it participates in EMU. Apart from the government, its other main customers include the commercial banks and foreign central banks. The Bank is sometimes known as 'The Old Lady of Threadneedle Street'.

bank statement   A document, issued by a bank to its customers, listing details of debit and credit transactions over a given period with a resultant balance of the account. These statements are issued to cover a range of accounts including current accounts, loan accounts and deposit accounts etc.

Bankers Automated Clearing Services   See BACS Limited.

banker's draft   In situations where a person owes money (particularly a large amount) to another who is not prepared to accept a personal cheque, the former can make the cheque payable to his/her bank. The bank in turn draws a cheque on itself (the banker's draft) which is submitted to the person to whom the sum is owed, which transaction is undisputed.

banker's reference   A reference sought from a bank by a company or individual regarding the creditworthiness of another company or individual in order to asses whether or not credit trading terms should be offered.

Banking Ombudsman [UK]   See Ombudsman.

bankruptcy   A situation where an individual is incapable of settling his/her debts and has been served a bankruptcy order by a court.

bargain   A term used on the LONDON STOCK EXCHANGE to describe a share purchase or sale. No special price is implied.

barter   An exchange of products or services between individuals without the involvement of money.

base metals   The main industrial non-ferrous metals excluding precious metals and minor metals. These are copper, primary aluminium, lead, nickel, tin and zinc. See London Metal Exchange.

base rate [UK]   The lowest rate at which a bank will charge interest. Typically, depending on the circumstances of the borrower, the bank will charge at some level above base rate. (for example, where base rate is 7% and interest charged is 9%, then it is said that interest is 2% above base rate and will continue at this difference as base rates vary unless renegotiated by the borrower.) The USA equivalent is PRIME RATE.

basic pension [UK]   The basic state pension funded by an individual's NATIONAL INSURANCE CONTRIBUTIONS over his/her working life.

basic rate tax   The main rate of INCOME TAX in the UK, currently 22%. There are two other rates that is, lower rate (10%) and higher rate (40%).

basic sum assured [UK]   A term used in conjunction with policies such as LOW COST ENDOWMENT ASSURANCE and LOW START ENDOWMENT ASSURANCE. Such policies operate on a 'with profits' basis and often in conjunction with repaying a loan such as a MORTGAGE. In the event of death during the term, a GUARANTEED DEATH BENEFIT repays the loan. However, to guarantee to pay the entire loan at maturity would incur very high premiums. Accordingly, a policy with lower premiums guarantees to repay only a proportion of the loan amount at maturity (the basic sum assured). The expectancy then is that the balance will be repaid by way of REVERSIONARY and (possibly) TERMINAL BONUSES.

basis   The difference between the price of a FUTURES contract and the spot or cash price. The item being traded may be a COMMODITY or a financial instrument.

bear   An investor who believes share prices are going to fall. He/she therefore sells shares in anticipation of buying them back at a lower price.

bear market   A market in which share prices are falling and in which a BEAR would profit.

bear spread   A strategy in OPTIONS trading in which an option is purchased at an EXERCISE PRICE above that of the UNDERLYING INSTRUMENT and simultaneously an option is sold at an exercise price below that of the underlying instrument, both with reference to the same expiry month. This applies to either CALL OPTIONS or PUT OPTIONS.

bearer bond   A bond which does not record its owner's name. Possession of the bond certificate is therefore the only proof of ownership. Dividends are claimed by submitting a detachable coupon to the paying agent.

bearer stocks/shares   Stocks or shares which do not record owner's names and issued by companies which do not keep a register of ownership. Possession of the certificate is therefore the only proof of ownership.

bed and breakfast [UK] A former practice of selling shares and their re-purchase the following day. This was based on the assumption it was unlikely that a share price would change very much from its afternoon value to the following morning. The purpose was to take advantage of CAPITAL GAINS TAX allowance. This strategy could be used to establish 1) a capital loss which could be offset against other gains or 2) a capital gain to lessen future liabilities. The March 1998 budget effectively ended bed and break-fasting by asserting that shares could not be repurchased within 30 days of being sold, for CGT purposes.

beneficial loan [UK]   A loan made by an employer to an employee on which interest is either not charged or is less than the official rate. The difference between the interest charged and the official rate is taxable.

beneficial owner   The true owner of a SECURITY or property which may be registered in another name. In the USA, when stocks are held by a broker in STREET NAME the true owner is the beneficial owner even though the broker holds title. In the UK the equivalent situation would be shares registered in a NOMINEE ACCOUNT.

beneficiary   **1.** A person who benefits from a trust set up on his/her behalf. **2.** Anyone who benefits from the proceeds of a will. **3.** A person who benefits from the proceeds of a life insurance policy.

Benefits Agency [UK] An executive agency within the DSS (Department of Social Security). The Benefits Agency is the provider of state pensions, child benefit, industrial injuries, disablement benefit and other social security benefits.

benefits in kind These are benefits, excluding salaries, given to employees which include cars and car fuel, medical insurance and gifts etc.

bequest The making of a gift by WILL. See legacy.

best advice [UK] A requirement of the 1986 Financial Services Act and in turn the FSA that a financial adviser, whether independent or a tied agent, must provide best advice regarding the most suitable product for a client having first established a full understanding of his/her financial background. An additional requirement is that recommendations should not be influenced by commissions payable.

Best's Ratings [USA] Ratings of financial reliability given by Best's Rating Service to insurance companies with a top rating of A++. This information is of importance to both buyers of insurance and investors in insurance stocks.

beta shares [UK] A term previously given to the shares of LISTED COMPANIES, basically second in line to and traded with less activity than ALPHA SHARES on the LONDON STOCK EXCHANGE, along with GAMMA and DELTA SHARES. These terms were replaced by the NORMAL MARKET SIZE classification in January 1991.

beta value A measurement of the movement of the price of a particular stock/share compared with the movement of the market as a whole. For example a stock with a beta value of one would be expected to move in line with an index such as the STANDARD AND POOR'S COMPOSITE INDEX (S&P 500) or the FTSE 100 INDEX. Beta values of less than one would imply less risk but less chance of gain. Beta values of greater than one imply more risk but more chance of gain.

bid The price which a purchaser is prepared to pay for an item.

bid price The price at which a MARKET MAKER will buy a security (stocks, shares, bonds etc) or a management company will buy back units in a UNIT TRUST from investors. See offer price.

bid and asked [USA] Bid is the highest price an investor is prepared to pay for a security. Asked is the lowest a seller is prepared to accept.

bid asked spread [USA]   The difference between the BID PRICE and asked price for a security. The two terms make up a QUOTATION.

bid/offer spread [UK]   The difference between the BID PRICE and the OFFER PRICE for shares and for units in a UNIT TRUST. It includes an allowance for the INITIAL CHARGE if there is one plus dealing costs.

Big Bang   A term referring to major operational changes on the LONDON STOCK EXCHANGE made on 27th October 1986. These included the introduction of MARKET MAKERS to combine the functions of stockbrokers and stockjobbers and the ending of fixed commissions.

Big Board   A popular name for the NEW YORK STOCK EXCHANGE.

billing cycle [USA]   The time between periodic billings for goods and services, typically one month.

bill of exchange (BE)   An order in writing by one person to another to pay a specified sum to a specified person or bearer on a particular date. The person making the order or drawing the bill is known as the drawer. The person to whom the bill is addressed is the drawee (for example a bank). The person to whom the bill is payable is the payee.

bill of sale   A formal document for the transference of title to goods from the seller to buyer.

bi-weekly mortgage loan [USA]   A MORTGAGE whereby the borrower makes a half monthly payment every two weeks instead of the usual 12 monthly payments. This arrangement results in 26 half monthly payments per year and a significant reduction in interest since an extra monthly payment is made, also an early repayment of the loan.

black knight   A company (or person) making an unwanted, hostile bid for another company. See grey knight. See white knight.

Black Monday   Monday 19th October 1987 when stockmarket values around the world fell heavily triggered by a large fall in the DOW JONES INDUSTRIAL AVERAGE in the USA.

blue chip   The stocks or shares of larger and well established corporations/companies which are sound and highly regarded for their quality products and their potential to pay dividends.

bona fide   A term meaning 'in good faith'. For example a person entering into an insurance contract is required to divulge all pertinent information in good faith. Failure to do so could result in breach of the contract and thus making it void. See uberrimae fidei.

bond   A fixed interest security issued by governments and corporations/ companies where guarantees are given to repay the capital and interest is paid at a rate as specified on the bond or policy document.

bond anticipation note (BAN) [USA]   A short term municipal or state note which is repaid from the proceeds of a forthcoming issue'.

bond discount   The difference between a bond's FACE VALUE and the MARKET PRICE. If the market price is higher than the face value, the difference is known as the bond premium. When interest rates rise, it is usual for bond prices to fall and when interest rates fall it is usual for bond prices to increase.

bond mutual fund [USA]   A MUTUAL FUND which invests in bonds which may be government, municipal or corporate etc.

bond rating [USA]   Ratings by various rating services regarding the likelihood of default by a bond issuer. These include Standard and Poor's and Moody's. Ratings range from AAA (highly regarded) to D (default).

bond yield   The return to an investor on the capital investment in a bond, that is, the interest paid expressed as a percentage of capital outlay. Where bonds are traded on a stock exchange, the yield will be dependent on the current purchase price and thus will vary. As the price of a bond falls, so the yield increases and vice versa.

bonus [USA]   A sum paid by a life insurance company to the INSURED based on investment proceeds. **[UK]** An additional sum paid on a WITH PROFITS assurance contract to policyholders. The amount is dependent on the profits of the assurance company. REVERSIONARY BONUSES are usually added annually whilst a TERMINAL BONUS may be payable at maturity or in the event of the death of the LIFE ASSURED.

bonus declaration [UK]   The declaration by a life company as to the rate of bonuses on a WITH PROFITS policy. REVERSIONARY BONUSES are normally paid annually and could typically be in the region of 2% to 5%. TERMINAL BONUSES (payable at maturity or prior death) tend to vary much more but could vary from say 10% to 100% at maturity depending on the term of the policy, for example ten and twenty five year terms.

bonus issue   See scrip issue.

book   A record maintained by a trading specialist of buy and sell orders for a given security.

book value   The value of an asset as entered in an organisation's BOOKS OF ACCOUNT.

books of account   The books in which the transactions of a business are recorded.

bought deal   The purchase of new shares by an underwriter who subsequently attempts to resell to the market for a profit.

bourse   A French or continental European stock exchange.

break even   The level of a company's sales at which neither a profit nor a loss is made.

break up value   A situation where a company, unable to continue trading, sells its assets individually to realise more value.

Bretton Woods Agreement   An agreement made in Bretton Woods, USA in 1944 which established a post war fixed currency rate between countries and subsequently the International Monetary Fund (IMF). The fixed exchange rate functioned until the early 1970's when it was replaced by a floating exchange rate.

bridge loan (bridging loan)   A short term loan, typically made by a bank to a customer in anticipation of a long term loan. For example, a bridge loan would be apt to purchase a property although the proceeds of the sale of an existing property and mortgage financing are still awaited.

broad money [UK]   See money supply M4.

broker   A business AGENT with specialist knowledge of a market, for example, STOCKBROKER and INSURANCE BROKER. Brokers offer advice to clients and are either paid by a fixed fee or by commission.

brokerage fee   Commission or fees charged by a broker for conducting transactions for its clients.

budget account   A bank account set up to control a person's regular expenditure. The account would typically include the payment of such items as mortgage, utilities, telephone and other similar items Annual expenditure for each item is divided by 12 and paid into the account monthly. The bills are then paid from the budget account as they become due.

Building Societies Investor Protection Scheme [UK]   A scheme set up to give limited protection to persons with share and/or deposit accounts in authorised building societies which fail. Building societies are regulated and supervised by the BUILDING SOCIETIES COMMISSION and the Scheme is operated by the Building Societies Investor Protection Board. In the case of an authorised building society being wound up there is a provision to pay compensation of 90% of a person's shares and/or deposits up to a set maximum.

building society [UK]   A non profit making institution whose principle purpose is making loans which are secured on residential property and funded substantially by its members. Building societies are currently regulated by the Building Societies Commission although this responsibility is passing to the FINANCIAL SERVICES AUTHORITY (FSA). See deposit account. See share account.

buildings insurance [UK]   Insurance which covers the policyholder against certain building losses or damages which may occur. The insurers will usually specify a maximum claim limit (the sum insured) which is the full rebuilding cost of the home. It is the owner's responsibility to ensure the sum insured is correct and to regularly update this cover. See contents insurance.

bull   An investor who believes prices of SHARES / COMMODITIES etc are going to rise. He/she is therefore a buyer in anticipation of selling at a higher price. See bear.

bull market   A market in which prices are rising and in which a BULL would profit. See bear market.

bull spread   A strategy in OPTIONS trading in which an option is purchased at an EXERCISE PRICE below that of the UNDERLYING INSTRUMENT and simultaneously an option is sold at an exercise price above that of the underlying instrument, both with reference to the same expiry month. This applies to both CALL OPTIONS or PUT OPTIONS.

bulldog bond   A bond issued on the UK market by a foreign institution.

bullion   Gold or silver in the form of ingots for bulk use.

bullion coins   Coins made from gold or silver. They can be easily traded.

Buyers Guide [UK]   A document, relevant to LIFE ASSURANCE, PERSONAL PENSION and UNIT TRUST products, which is given to prospective clients at the initial interview, which indicates that the adviser is either independent or a TIED AGENT (COMPANY REPRESENTATIVE) and how they differ. The guide subsequently states the identity of the issuer that is, which type of adviser he/she is and his/her obligations to the investor. Also the company whose products may be purchased will provide full product details and indications of charges/ commissions payable in writing. It is a mandatory requirement, whether advisers are independent or tied agents, that a Buyers Guide be given to a prospective client (PROSPECT) prior to any product discussions.

bylaws [USA] The rules under which a corporation's internal management operates. They include details such as election of directors, duties of officers and how share transfers can be conducted. See articles of incorporation.

C

cafeteria employee benefit plan [USA]   A plan enabling employees to choose from a variety of benefits, depending on their own particular circumstances. Young employees for example will have different requirements to older employees.

call [USA] The redeeming of a BOND by an issuer before its maturity date. **[UK] 1.** A demand by a company to shareholders to pay a further instalment on partly paid shares. **2.** A demand by a bank for the full repayment of a loan when the borrower has failed to meet his/her obligations under the terms of the loan agreement.

call date [USA]   The date on which a BOND may be redeemed by the issuer before maturity which may be at par or at a higher value. The difference is known as the call premium.

call option   An OPTION which gives the HOLDER the right but not the obligation to purchase a stated quantity of the UNDERLYING INSTRUMENT (for example shares, indices, commodities etc) at a specified price on or before a given date. See put option.

call price [USA]   The price at which a BOND or PREFERRED STOCK can be redeemed by the issuer. The call price will usually be greater than the par value to compensate the holder for loss of income and ownership. The difference is known as the call premium.

call provision [USA]   A provision of a BOND or PREFERRED STOCK issue, listed in its INDENTURE (the formal agreement between the bond issuer and the holder) that allows the issuer to redeem the bond before the maturity date either at par or at a premium to par.

cancel 1. To make an agreement void. **2. [USA]** The voiding of a buy or sell order.

cancellation notice [UK]   A notice which must be given to investors entering into long term insurance contracts informing them they have the right to cancel within 14 days of receipt of the notice.

---

cancellation price [UK]   The lowest possible BID PRICE of units in a UNIT TRUST under FSA regulations which is usually lower than the quoted bid price. The cancellation price may be applied in the event of heavy selling.

capital   1. The overall assets of an individual less liabilities. **2.** Money injected into a company by way of SHARE CAPITAL and LOAN CAPITAL plus RETAINED EARNINGS.

capital allowance [UK]   A tax allowance which takes account of depreciation of certain types of business assets such as plant and machinery and motor vehicles etc.

capital assets   Assets, purchased as a long term investment for generating profit, such as buildings, plant and machinery and fixtures etc.

capital employed   Capital used to produce profit.

capital expenditure   A company's expenditure to acquire CAPITAL ASSETS.

capital gain   The difference between the selling price of an asset and the buying price.

capital gains tax (CGT)   A tax imposed on the profits from the sale of assets. In the USA, if the HOLDING PERIOD of the asset is over one year, tax treatment of any gain is more favourable. In the UK, gains are taxed after taking into consideration an annual capital gains allowance after which a 'tapering' of CGT is introduced. This allows a tapering reduction of tax rates over the longer term.

capital gearing   See gearing.

capital growth   Capital assets, for example shares or a house, which increase in value.

capital movement   See balance of payments.

capital shares [USA]   Shares which entitle the holder to receive the capital appreciation from a DUAL PURPOSE FUND. The other type of shares in such a fund are INCOME SHARES which receive the fund's income. In the UK this type of fund is called a SPLIT CAPITAL INVESTMENT TRUST. **[UK] 1.** Shares which entitle the holder to receive the capital appreciation from the portfolio of a split capital investment trust. **2.**   Shares whose value to an investor are expected to be by way of significant share price increase rather than payment of income.

capital structure [USA]   The components which form a corporation's capital that is, COMMON STOCK, LONG TERM DEBT and PREFERRED STOCK. **[UK]** The components which together form a company's capital. These include ORDINARY SHARES, PREFERENCE SHARES, DEBENTURES and LOAN STOCK.

capitalisation   **1.** The injection of capital into a company. **2.** See capital structure. **3.** The reserves of a company which are converted into additional shares for shareholders.

capitalisation issue   See scrip issue.

car benefit [UK]   Where a company provides an employee with a company motor car which is used privately in addition to company business, a tax liability may arise which will depend on a number of factors including salary and motor car details such as cost, age, engine capacity etc. A company director provided with a company car will be liable for tax irrespective of salary.

carat   A measurement unit defining the purity of gold. Pure gold is 24 carat, whilst 18 carat gold comprises 18/24 gold and 6/24 alloy.

carry back [UK]   A term applicable to personal pensions regarding tax rules which allow contributions made in the current tax year to be treated as though they were paid in the preceding tax year. If there were no NET RELEVANT EARNINGS in the preceding year, the contribution can be carried back a further year. The advantage of taking up this choice is that tax relief is obtained at the highest rate applicable in that previous year. For example, if an individual's earnings have fallen such that he/she is no longer a higher rate taxpayer, carry back of contributions will obtain tax relief at the highest rate.

carry forward [UK]   A term applicable to personal pensions regarding tax rules which allow an individual to make contributions, additional to the current tax year, for the six previous years where maximum contributions have not been made. However, before the carry forward rules apply, maximum contributions must first be paid for the current tax year.

cash   Money, in the form of notes and coins, which constitutes payment for goods at the time of purchase.

cash and carry   An ARBITRAGE transaction applied on a FUTURES market where the cash or SPOT PRICE of for example, a COMMODITY is less than the FUTURES CONTRACT price. Under these circumstances a purchase of the cash commodity with borrowed money and the simultaneous sale of the futures contract can provide a profit.

cash card   See ATM card.

cash dividend [USA]   A payment of a proportion of a corporation's profits to shareholders in the form of cash. An alternative form of payment is by way of stock, that is, a STOCK DIVIDEND. In the UK cash dividends are known simply as dividends. When a company pays a dividend in the form of shares it is sometimes known as a SCRIP DIVIDEND.

cash dispenser   See automated teller machine.

cash flow   The measure of cash received and cash spent by a company, institution or individual.

cash market   An expression used to describe the market in the UNDERLYING INSTRUMENT (for example, shares, indices, commodities, etc.) on which a FUTURES or OPTIONS contract is based. Also known as SPOT or PHYSICAL market. In a cash market the commodity or financial instrument is transferred from seller to buyer.

cash settlement   **1.** Deals on an exchange where investors are obliged to settle immediately rather than on account. **2.** An expression used in FUTURES and OPTIONS trading which applies when physical delivery is impractical and contracts are settled by attaching a monetary value.

cash surrender value [USA]   The value of funds returnable to the INSURED from the INSURER upon the surrender of a CASH VALUE LIFE INSURANCE policy.

cash value life insurance [USA]   A LIFE INSURANCE policy which pays a benefit on the death of the INSURED but which also provides a savings element where benefits are payable before death.

casualty insurance [USA]   Insurance which gives protection to a business or homeowner against property loss, damage and injury to a third party.

caveat emptor Latin for 'let the buyer beware'. This implies a buyer must ensure that goods about to be pur-chased are free from defects and that he/she bears the risk.

Central Register [UK] A computerised database of some 50,000 investment firms which have been authorised to conduct investment business by one of the investment regulatory watchdogs such as the PERSONAL INVESTMENT AUTHORITY (PIA). The Register is maintained by the senior investment regulator, the FINANCIAL SERVICES AUTHORITY (FSA) and enables the public to check whether a firm is authorised. Information listed includes the name, address and telephone number of each firm's main place of business.

certificate of deduction of tax [UK] A certificate, issued by a building society or bank (in accordance with Section 352 of the Income and Corporation Taxes Act 1988) to its customers with interest bearing accounts, in which gross interest, tax deducted and net interest are depicted.

certificate of deposit A certificate, issued by a bank to a depositor, indicating a sum of money has been deposited for a specified term and on which interest is paid.

charge card A plastic payment card enabling the holder to obtain goods and services without the requirement to pay cash. Accounts are normally submitted to the card holder monthly and must be settled in full. In addition to obtaining goods, the charge card can be used to obtain cash. Examples of charge cards are AMERICAN EXPRESS, DINERS CLUB and a number of gold cards. See also credit card and debit card.

chargeable event [UK] A transaction which leads to a CHARGEABLE GAIN and which in turn promotes the issuing of a CHARGEABLE EVENT CERTIFICATE. For example the sale of an investment bond with a life company which results in a gain will be classed as a chargeable event.

chargeable event certificate [UK] A certificate issued on the occurrence of a CHARGEABLE EVENT. Details listed include the amount of the gain, number of years over which the gain has occurred, the date the transaction took place and that the certificate should be sent to the Tax Office to establish if a higher rate tax liability exists. Proceeds are free from basic rate tax liability.

chargeable gain [UK] The amount of a gain which may incur a tax liability.

charity An organisation whose aim is to provide help for the needy. Trusts which are registered with the appropriate authority can receive legacies from a deceased person's estate free of inheritance tax.

charitable trust A trust which has been registered with the appropriate authority and which enjoys income tax advantages.

chartist An analyst who uses graphs relating to past performance of securities etc. to anticipate future trends.

chattels A term used in wills which refers to the personal possessions of the maker of the WILL. Such items would typically be jewellery, furniture, books, tools and private motor cars etc.

check [USA] cheque [UK] A printed form on which a written order is given to a person's or company's bank to pay a specific sum to a named recipient or bearer.

check card [USA] cheque card [UK] A card, issued by a bank (or a building society in the UK), which guarantees the payment of a check to the recipient and which supports a check for obtaining cash, both up to a stated value.

check clearing [USA] cheque clearing [UK] A system which enables checks to be transmitted between banks (and between branches) in order to transfer funds.

checking account [USA] cheque account [UK] An account, with a bank (or additionally a BUILDING SOCIETY in the UK) into which deposits are made and from which payments are made by check. See also DEPOSIT ACCOUNT.

child deferred endowment [UK] An ENDOWMENT ASSURANCE, on the life of a child, which can be taken as cash at MATURITY or converted to a FULL ENDOWMENT or WHOLE LIFE ASSURANCE.

Citizens Advice Bureau An office, represented in most towns in the UK, where the public can obtain free advice on an extensive range of civil matters including social security, consumer matters such as loans and rental arrears, employment, housing matters such as mortgage and rent arrears, legal matters such as legal aid, family matters, taxation and many other subjects.

claim A demand by the INSURED for a benefit to be paid by the insurers under the conditions of the policy.

Class 1, 2, 3 and 4 National Insurance Contributions [UK] See National Insurance Contributions.

clawback [UK] 1. A term used in life assurance where under certain conditions, LIFE ASSURANCE PREMIUM RELIEF (LAPR) given under a life policy could be recovered (or clawed back) by the Inland Revenue. Although not extinct the situation has much less relevance in the 90's. **2.** Where a life company advances INDEMNITY COMMISSION to an agent, the company does so on the understanding it will be entitled to take back some or all (clawback) such commission if the relevant policy is cancelled within a given period.

clearing **1.** The process of moving payments between accounts from different banks or branches. **2. [UK]** A term used on FUTURES and OPTIONS exchanges which refers to the process of registration, settlement and provision of a guarantee of exchange traded transactions.

clearing corporation [USA], clearing house [UK] An independent organisation, appointed by an exchange, which guarantees securities transactions.

client agreement A document issued by an adviser/broker to a client outlining the basis of the relationship and the services for which the adviser/broker is authorised. This is required when a relationship is of a continuing nature.

close market [USA] A securities market in which the difference between bid and offer prices is narrow and which depicts high volume trading.

close out A FUTURES transaction where an equal and opposite trade closes an OPEN POSITION. This leaves a trader with what is known as a zero net position.

closed corporation [USA] A corporation in which publicly held shares are owned by only a few individuals and not usually available for trading.

closed end fund A fund which has a fixed number of shares which are normally be traded on a stock exchange where prices are affected by supply and demand. See open end fund.

closely held corporation [USA] A corporation with only a small number of shareholders. Although a public com-pany, shares would not normally be available for trading.

closing purchase The purchase of an OPTION, by a WRITER, which has the same terms as an option which has previously been sold. This transaction terminates his/her obligations as a writer.

closing range A FUTURES expression which refers to a range of closely allied prices at which transactions were conducted at the close of a trading day.

closing sale The sale of an OPTION, by a HOLDER, identical to the option which is held. This transaction terminates his/her rights as a holder.

codicil A document on which changes or additions are made to an existing signed will. Both the will and the codicil must be read in conjunction with one another.

cold calling An approach by a salesperson to a prospect (prospective buyer) either by telephone or in person where no previous contact has been made. In the UK, when cold calling in respect of life assurance, pensions and unit trusts, a code of practice must be followed by the salesperson which includes the declaration of the name of the caller and his/her company and the purpose of the call etc.

collateral An asset pledged as a guarantee to a lender until a loan is repaid. An example is a life insurance policy which has acquired a CASH SURRENDER VALUE equal or greater in value to the loan amount.

collecting branch A banking term which refers to the branch which accepts cheques to be credited to its customers' accounts and subsequently obtains the proceeds from the issuing banks, usually by a clearing arrangement.

COMEX Formerly an abbreviation for the Commodity Exchange in New York and now a division of the NEW YORK MERCANTILE EXCHANGE after its merger with NYMEX. It is the main US market for metals FUTURES and OPTIONS trading in copper, gold and silver.

commercial bank [UK] A bank, such as Barclays, Lloyds, which provides services to companies and individuals in the form of current, deposit and loan accounts plus a variety of other financial services including mortgages, insurance and financial planning etc.

commercial mortgage A MORTGAGE on a non residential building within which a business operates.

commercial paper [USA] A short term NOTE issued by banks and corporations with a range of maturities from 30 days to 270 days.

commission Payment made to an AGENT for his/her part in the sale of products to a client or customer. The payment is invariably made to the agent by his/her PRINCIPAL, that is, the originator of the product.

commodity (commodities) Basic raw materials and foodstuffs such as metals, petroleum, coffee, grain etc. An article of trade as opposed to a service. Commodities are traded on a commodity exchange. In the USA, commodities of various types are traded on a number of exchanges including the Chicago Board of Trade, Chicago Mercantile Exchange,

Kansas City Board of Trade and Mid America Commodity Exchange. In the UK, commodities are traded on the London Metal Exchange, the International Petroleum Exchange and The London International Financial Futures and Options Exchange which incorporates the London Commodity Exchange.

commodity broker   A broker who deals in COMMODITIES in a commodities market.

common stock [USA]   A share in a public or private company where the holder is an owner in the company.   He/she is entitled to vote on the election of directors and to receive a dividend in relation to the extent of his/her stock holding.   Holders of common stock will also seek to enhance the capital value of their investment by way of stock price increase over the longer term.   In the event of the company being wound up holders of common stock are the last in line to be paid.   Similar to an ordinary share in the UK.

common stock fund [USA]   A MUTUAL FUND which invests solely in common stocks of companies.

community charge [UK]   A charge, levied on all adult citizens in the UK, which replaced the previous rates system for council finance.   The charge was unpopular and was subsequently replaced by the COUNCIL TAX on 1st April 1993.

community property [USA]   Property owned by a married couple and held jointly.

commutation [UK]   A term used to describe a person's right to convert part of his/her PENSION fund into cash (tax free) at retirement age at the expense of a reduced pension.   See occupational pension scheme.   See personal pension plan.

company doctor   A business executive specializing in rectifying the problems of companies in difficulties.

company pension   See occupational pension scheme.

company representative (tied agent) [UK]   The representative of a particular company, authorised to give FINANCIAL ADVICE in products such as LIFE ASSURANCE, PENSIONS and UNIT TRUSTS.   Such a representative may recommend products from that company only.   Under the FINANCIAL SERVICES ACT 1986 all financial advisers must declare to the client whether they are a company representative/tied agent or INDEPENDENT FINANCIAL

ADVISER (IFA) and they must present to the client a BUYERS GUIDE prior to any product discussions. Companies which market products supported by company representatives are mainly regulated by the PERSONAL INVESTMENT AUTHORITY (PIA).

compensating balance [USA] The balance required to be kept on deposit at a bank by a borrower when taking out a loan. Should the borrower fail to repay the loan either in full or in part, this balance would be forfeited. Compensating balances are typically 10% of the loan amount.

compliance [USA] Procedures adopted by stock exchanges to oversee trading to ensure compliance with the SECURITIES AND EXCHANGE COMMISSION rules. **[UK]** Procedures that must be adopted by life companies, their representatives and independent intermediaries, as a result of the FINANCIAL SERVICES ACT 1986. Life companies each appoint a compliance officer to ensure that compliance procedures are followed.

compound interest Interest, which is earned on the principal over a given period (for example, one year), is added to the principal and in subsequent periods the principal plus interest earn further interest.

For example:
Principal = $1,000.
Compound interest paid annually at 5%
At end of first year, principal + interest =
$1,000.00 + $50.00 = $1,050.00
At end of second year, (principal + interest) + interest
= $1,050.00 + $52.50 = $1,102.50

compound reversionary bonus [UK] A WITH PROFITS life assurance bonus, normally added annually to the policy, which is based on the profits of the life company's invest-ments. The compound reversionary bonus is normally calculated on the SUM ASSURED (or BASIC SUM ASSURED) plus bonuses to date and is payable at the maturity of the policy or prior death. Once declared, reversionary bonuses are guaranteed.

comprehensive insurance A term used to describe an insurance policy in which a wide range of risks are covered, an example being comprehensive motor insurance.

compulsory purchase annuity See annuity.

Confederation of British Industry (CBI) An independent non-profit making, non party political organ-isation which represents the interests of 250,000 direct and indirect member companies in the UK. The CBI was founded in 1965 by the merging of the Federation of British Industries, the British Employers' Confederation and the National Association of British Manufacturers. Finance is provided by members' subscriptions and a range of other commercial activities including conferences and publications and the membership includes companies of all sizes from all sectors of industry and commerce. The organisation's objective is to develop the conditions necessary for UK businesses to be competitive and to prosper. Close liaison is maintained with the government regarding its members' views and increasingly with Brussels and Strasbourg.

conglomerate   A company which owns a number of other companies with widely diversified activities.

consideration   Something of value given by one party to another in return for entering into a contract. **[UK]** The money value of a LONDON STOCK EXCHANGE transaction (the value of the sale of a security) excluding costs such as charges and STAMP DUTY etc.

consols   See irredeemable stocks.

constant dollar plan [USA]   A plan which enables investors to accumulate shares in stock or a MUTUAL FUND by purchasing on a regular basis (for example monthly) with a fixed dollar amount. When the price is low, more shares will be purchased and fewer when the price is high. Also known as dollar cost averaging. Known as pound cost averaging in the UK.

consumer durables   A product such as an automobile or appliance whose life expectancy is at least three years.

consumer price index (CPI) [USA]   An index which tracks the prices of a variety of goods purchased by an average consumer. The goods typically include food, clothing, utilities and medical care. Also known as the cost of living index which is used as a reference for wage increases and other similar inflation prone items such as Social Security payments.

contango   A situation in FUTURES trading where the future delivery price is greater than the cash or nearby price.

contents insurance [UK]   Insurance which gives cover in respect of the contents of a home. This includes damage, theft or loss to items such as carpets, furniture, freezer contents, jewellery and cash etc. It is usual for the insurers to specify a maximum claim limit for each section of items covered. This information is listed on the policy schedule issued by the insurers. Contents insurance can be linked with BUILDINGS INSURANCE in a combined policy provided by a single company. See household insurance.

contingent assurance [UK] LIFE ASSURANCE where payment of the SUM ASSURED depends on an event or events additional to the death of the LIFE ASSURED. For example the policy may specify the prior death of the spouse of the life assured.

contingent liabilities Liabilities (debts) that may or may not be incurred by a company and which depend on the outcome of say a forthcoming event such as a court case. These are recorded in a company's accounts as contingent liabilities.

contra An entry made into an account or statement to nullify a previous entry.

contract 1. A legal agreement between two or more persons. **2. [UK]** The minimum amount of a COMMODITY or financial instrument in which trading may take place. Also known as a lot.

contract month The specified month to which a FUTURES or OPTIONS contract refers. This is the month when the specified instrument is delivered in exchange for CASH SETTLEMENT.

contract note A confirming note, containing details of a stock exchange deal, which is sent from a member firm to its client. The details include the date and time of deal, title of the security, price, consideration (the money value of the transaction) stamp duty (if applicable) and commission etc.

contract of insurance A contract between an insurer and the insured. The insurer agrees to pay money to the insured upon the occasion of given events in return for a single premium or regular premiums.

contracting out [UK] A term which refers to contracting out of SERPS (STATE EARNINGS RELATED PENSION SCHEME). A person can contract out by joining an employer's pension scheme which itself is contracted out or through an APPROPRIATE PERSONAL PENSION PLAN. The result of making this choice is that the person's SERPS pension will be reduced at retirement but there will now be the proceeds from the alternative pension plan selected.

Contributions Agency [UK]   An executive agency within the DSS (Department of Social Security). The Contributions Agency deals with all aspects of NI (National Insurance) contributions. The agency has locations throughout the country

contributions waiver benefit   See waiver of premium.

convergence   The movement of a FUTURES price towards that of the UNDERLYING INSTRUMENT as the contract date approaches.

conversion terms   **1.** The terms which apply when convertible loan stock, for example, a BOND or a DEBENTURE, are converted into ORDINARY SHARES or PREFERENCE SHARES. These would include the price and date of conversion which are fixed at the issue date. **2.** The terms which apply when a WARRANT is converted into shares. These would include the exercise price, the date or period of conversion and the number of shares (normally one per warrant) which the warrant holder would be entitled to purchase.

convertible [USA]   A BOND or PREFERRED STOCK which can be converted into COMMON STOCK at a given price. **[UK]**   A bond or DEBENTURE which may be converted into ORDINARY SHARES or PREFERENCE SHARES at a given price at a future date.

convertible term insurance [USA]   TERM LIFE INSURANCE which can be converted into CASH VALUE INSURANCE. In the UK the equivalent (convertible term assurance) is conversion of TERM ASSURANCE into ENDOWMENT ASSURANCE.

conveyancing [UK]   The business of the legal transfer of real PROPERTY from one owner to another.

cooling off period [UK]   The 14 day period during which a new policyholder can cancel an insurance/assurance policy. This is referred to in the CANCELLATION NOTICE which must be sent to persons entering into long term policies. The 14 day period starts from receipt of the cancellation notice.

cooperative   A business owned and operated by its members.

corporate bond [USA]   A debt security issued by a company. The par value, usually $1,000 is repayable at maturity. Interest is payable at regular intervals throughout the life of the bond. Corporate bonds are tradeable on major stock exchanges.

corporate bond PEP [UK]   See personal equity plan.

corporation tax [UK]   A tax payable by a company on its profits.

cost basis   The cost price of an asset used to establish CAPITAL GAINS TAX liability.

cost of sales   The cost to a company of producing goods. Similarly with a retailer or distributor type business, cost of sales is the cost of purchasing goods prior to their resale.

council tax [UK]   A local taxation system which was introduced on 1st April 1993 to replace the previous and unpopular community charge (poll tax). The tax is based on the property value and the assumption that there are two or more adults in residence (aged over 18). There are eight bands of property values (A to H) and the tax incurred by each dwelling increases in increments from band A to band H. There is no further charge if there are more than two persons resident but if the dwelling is only occupied by one individual, the bill will receive a discount.**coupon**   The rate of interest paid by the issuer of a bond until maturity.

coupon bond   See bearer bond.

court of protection [UK]   A office of the Supreme Court whose function is to manage and administer the property and affairs of persons who, through mental disorder, are incapable of managing their own financial affairs.

covenant   A formal agreement made in a DEED.

cover [USA]   The net asset value underlying a bond or stock. **[UK] 1.** The ratio between a company's net profit after tax and the dividend paid to its shareholders.
For example:
Net profit after tax (earnings) = £700,000.00 Dividend paid = £300,000.00
The cover is £700,000.00 / £300,000.00 = 2.33 times.

Cover indicates a company's capability to continue its dividend payment and can also be viewed as its commitment to investment for future growth. In the USA the reverse ratio is used, that is, dividend payment divided by net earnings, known as DIVIDEND PAYOUT RATIO. This gives the percentage of earnings paid to shareholders. **2.** The details of insurance provided by an insurance company to the policyholder.

credit   1. A sum of money entered into a bank or financial institution account thereby improving the balance. **2.** Included in the trading terms between companies, credit is the value of goods which one company will supply to another before payment is necessary.

credit bureau An agency which accumulates credit information relative to the credit reliability of consumers and subsequently makes such information available at a fee to companies offering credit terms.

credit card A plastic payment card which allows the owner to obtain goods and services without the requirement to pay cash and on credit terms. Transactions during a month are totalled and presented to the card holder for settlement on a monthly basis. Alternatively a percentage of the outstanding amount can be paid and the balance extended to the next month and so on. This will normally incur a much higher annual rate of interest than usual, for example, 2% per month being equivalent to an ANNUAL PERCENTAGE RATE of 26.82%. In addition to obtaining goods, the credit card can be used to obtain cash. See also charge card and debit card.

credit clearing A system for the distribution of bank giro credits and other credits between banks to enable funds to be transferred into specified accounts.

credit control Methods used by companies to try to ensure their customers pay their accounts/bills within the agreed time period.

credit note A note, issued to a person or company when goods are returned by them, which cancels the original invoice. If the invoice has been settled before the goods are returned the credit note will then entitle the holder to alternative goods (or sometimes cash) to the original value.

credit union A mutual association formed by persons with a common affiliation such as employees, a union or a religious group in which pooled saving are made. The funds are invested for appreciation and members may borrow at competitive rates.

creditors Persons or companies to whom monies are owed. Thus a company's creditors are those to whom payment is to be made. See DEBTORS.

CREST An electronic system of SETTLEMENT for the securities/equities market in the UK and Ireland. Following the cancellation of the TAURUS project in 1993, the Bank of England initiated the design and the building of CREST to ensure faster, cheaper and more efficient paperless settlement. The system went live on 15th July 1996 and finally replaced the TALISMAN paper system during April 1997. CREST is owned and operated by CRESTCo.

critical illness cover   Insurance which covers the insured against specified critical illnesses such as cancer, heart attack and multiple sclerosis etc. In the event that the insured contracts one of the specified illnesses, the insurers would pay a lump sum rather than an income as in the case of PERMANENT HEALTH INSURANCE.

Crown [UK]   A term sometimes used in wills which effectively means HM Treasury. In the event of a deceased person not having made a will (INTESTACY), the proceeds from the estate pass to the Crown.

cum   A word meaning 'with'. Thus, for example, cum dividend means with dividend.

cumulative preference shares [UK]   When a company fails to pay a dividend, holders of cumulative preference shares are entitled to receive this missed payment when next a dividend is declared. This rule is cumulative and they are also entitled to the current dividend provided sufficient cash is available. These payments receive priority before the holders of ordinary shares.

cumulative preferred stock [USA]   Preferred stock with dividend payment priority following a missed dividend payment. This amount accumulates with subsequent dividends and when next a dividend is declared no payments can be made to common stockholders until cumulative preferred stockholders have been paid in full.

curb [USA]   The AMERICAN STOCK EXCHANGE which was originally known as the Curb Exchange.

currency   Cash, cheques etc. which circulate in an economy as an accepted means of exchange.

currency loan   A term used when money is borrowed in a foreign currency.

current account 1.   A BALANCE OF PAYMENTS account listing transactions other than capital movement.   **2.**   An account listing transactions between trading companies. **3.**   A bank account which offers a number of facilities including cheque book for debt settlement, deposits, direct debits and where applicable, OVERDRAFTS. This type of account is normally used for ongoing transactions (for example monthly direct debits and writing of cheques etc.) as opposed to a DEPOSIT ACCOUNT.

current assets   Assets of a company which are regularly turned over including cash, work in progress and debtors (monies owed to the company).

current income [USA]   Interest, dividend or other income payments received regularly from an investment source.

current liabilities   Debts owed by a company which are due for settlement within 12 months. These include CREDITORS (monies owed by the company) and taxes due etc.

current ratio   Current assets divided by current liabilities. This ratio gives an indication of a company's capability to pay its debts and as a broad rule should be one or more.

current yield   See yield.

Customs and Excise [UK]   See Her Majesty's Customs and Excise.

cyclical stock   Stock in companies whose profits are inclined to move in a cyclical manner, normally in phase with the economy. When prosperous times prevail profits increase but they decrease when the economy declines.

D

Daily Official List [UK]   The daily record of listed securities and price transactions published by the LONDON STOCK EXCHANGE.

data base   A structured set of data sorted in various configurations and stored in a computer.

dated security   A fixed interest SECURITY which has a specified date for repayment (redemption date).

date of record [USA]   The date by which a shareholder must own shares in order to qualify for a dividend.

day order   An order placed with a broker to purchase or sell stock, a COMMODITY or financial instrument at specified price limits.   If not executed that day the order becomes invalid.

day trade [USA]   The purchase and sale of a SECURITY on the same day.

days of grace   Additional days which may be allowed by a company to a DEBTOR over and above the due date for payment.   For example, a life insurance company may allow days of grace for a policy to be kept in force after the date the PREMIUM is due for payment.

deal   A transaction on a stock exchange by a broker or institution etc.

dealing   See DEAL.

death and superannuation benefit [UK]   An income tax allowance which can be claimed if certain payments are being made to friendly societies on combined sickness and life insurance policies. The allowance is half of the death benefit part of the premium. Also, relief is obtainable on trade union contributions which relate to superannuation, life insurance or funeral benefits. The allowance is half of the premium. Allowances for superannuation contributions to retirement benefit schemes are usually deducted by the employer before assessing tax on the remaining pay.

death benefit   The amount payable by a life insurance company to the BENEFICIARIES on the death of the insured (the policyholder). In the US this is the face value of the policy less any outstanding policy loans.

death duties [UK]   Tax payable on a deceased person's ESTATE. ESTATE TAX in the USA.

death in service   A life insurance policy which often attaches to a company pension scheme. The member is typically covered for three times his/her salary whilst remaining in the employ of the company and should death occur during this period (death in service), his/her dependants would receive the insured sum free of tax.

debenture   In the USA an unsecured bond. In the UK a type of loan, taken out by a company, normally to be repaid at a specified future date and with a fixed rate of interest. It is usual for the debenture to be secured against certain of the company's assets, that is, if the company fails to fulfil its interest payments and/or repayment of the loan when due, those assets are liable to be transferred to the lender.

debit   An outflow of funds from an account with a bank or financial institution. For example: When a person writes a cheque, his/her account will subsequently be debited with the amount.

debit card   A plastic payment card, issued by a bank or other financial institution, which enables the holder to obtain goods and services without the requirement to pay cash. The debiting procedure commences directly after the transaction which results in the holder's account being debited within a few days. In addition to obtaining goods, the card can be used to obtain cash which results in the holder's account being debited immediately. See also charge card and credit card.

debit note   A note, issued to a person or company indicating an amount owed. A more popular method of debiting is by an INVOICE.

debt   Money owed by an individual or company to another individual or company.

debt instrument   A promise in writing to repay a debt. For example a bond, bill or note.

debt security   A SECURITY such as a bond or note with specified interest, representing a loan which is repayable at some future date.

debt to equity ratio   The total liabilities of a company divided by stockholders' equity.

debtor   A person or company owing money to another person or company. A company is therefore owed money by its debtors and those to whom monies are owed are known as its CREDITORS.

declaration date   The date on which a dividend is declared by a company's directors. Once declared the dividend becomes a liability of the company.

decreasing term life insurance   Life insurance in which the death benefit decreases over the term of the policy although the premiums remain fixed. In the UK this is known as decreasing term assurance.

deductible **1.** An amount (normally fixed) a policyholder is obliged to pay prior to an insurance company paying a claim. **2. [USA]** An expense allowed as a deduction from ADJUSTED GROSS INCOME to reduce taxable income. For example, mortgage interest and state and local taxes.

deduction [USA]   An expense allowed by the INTERNAL REVENUE SERVICE which is deducted from ADJUSTED GROSS INCOME to establish TAXABLE INCOME. These include interest payments and state and local taxes. Known as an allowance in the UK. **[UK]** In the UK a deduction is an item which may be additive to income (such as a percentage of the value of a company vehicle). Deductions are subtracted from ALLOWANCES to give tax free pay.

deed   A document, which legally transfers ownership of property from one party another, more commonly related to real estate.

deed of covenant [UK]   A legal document, detailed in which is a specified sum of money to be transferred from one individual to another for a specified number of years, in order to save income tax. The individual making the payment deducts tax at the basic rate and thus pays a net amount on which tax relief is obtained. If the recipient is a registered charity the payer may obtain tax relief up to his/her higher rate whilst the charity can claim back the amount deducted.

default   Failure by a debtor to meet the terms of a loan such as non payment of interest and capital.

defeasance   The process of rendering a contract or deed null and void following a specified act.

defensive securities Securities which are considered to be more stable in price in a market where prices are falling.

deferment period [UK] A term used, for example, in PERMANENT HEALTH INSURANCE which refers to a period, prior to payment by the insurers to the policyholder after a claim, during which no payments are made. For example, a typical deferment period could be six months so if a policyholder made a claim after contracting an illness which qualified, it would be six months later that payments would commence. Sometimes an employee's company will continue paying his/her salary during this period so it would be important to ensure that the permanent health insurance links in timewise with the company's payment commitments. Also, as the deferment period increases so the premiums decrease.

deferred annuity See annuity.

deferred income [UK] Also known as income drawdown and flexible pension. See personal pension plan.

deferred state pension [UK] When reaching retirement age, a person can elect to defer payment of his/her state pension. The result of this is to increase the value of the pension by one seventh of one percent for every week deferred. The maximum deferment period is five years and no further contributions are required.

defined benefit pension plan A PENSION plan in which an employee's PENSION benefit is related to number of years service and FINAL SALARY with each employer.

defined contribution pension plan A PENSION plan in which benefits are dependent on contributions to and the growth of the pension fund.

deflation An economic situation in which there is a general fall in the level of prices.

delinquency [USA] Failure to make payment on a loan obligation on the due date.

delivery 1. The transfer of title of a security such as stock from buyer to seller. **2.** Settlement of a FUTURES CONTRACT by receipt or tender of a financial instrument (for example stock) or a COMMODITY or by cash settlement.

delivery month See contract month.

delta   The movement of an OPTION price relative to a change in the UNDERLYING INSTRUMENT (for example shares or a commodity).

delta shares [UK]   A term previously given to the shares of smaller companies least traded on the LONDON STOCK EXCHANGE, along with ALPHA, BETA and GAMMA shares. These terms were replaced by the normal market size classification in January 1991.

demand loan [USA]   A loan which the lender can recall at any time. There is no specific maturity date.

demand deposit [USA]   A bank account balance to which the holder has instant access. The holder can withdraw funds by check or cash.

demutualise   The conversion of a MUTUAL COMPANY to a proprietary company, that is, a company with shareholders.

denomination   The face value of currency coins and stocks and bonds.

dental insurance   Insurance which covers dental treatment in return for regular premiums.

deposit taking business   Money placed with financial institutions such as banks to attract INTEREST.

deposit account   An account, with a bank or financial institution, which earns interest normally proportional to and below current base rates. The notice period for withdrawal will also affect the interest rate. No cheque book is issued with a deposit account.

Deposit Protection Scheme [UK]   A scheme set up to give limited financial protection to persons with deposits in authorised banks which fail. Banks are authorised and supervised by the FINANCIAL SERVICES AUTHORITY (FSA) and they are obliged to provide details of their deposit protection scheme and their claim procedures if requested by depositors. The FSA publishes a list of banks which are authorised under the 1987 Banking Act. The UK Deposit Protection Scheme covers 90% of a bank's total liability to a depositor subject to a set maximum.

deposit insurance [USA]   Financial protection of certain bank and credit union accounts by way of insurance provided by a federal agency. Bank insurance up to specified limits is provided for funds on deposit in member banks by the FEDERAL DEPOSIT INSURANCE CORPORATION. CREDIT UNIONS which are federally chartered are insured by the NATIONAL CREDIT UNION ADMINISTRATION.

depreciation   The charge, as recorded in a company's accounts, which depicts the reduction in value of an asset.

depression   A severe RECESSION over a lengthened period.

derivatives   A collective term for FUTURES and OPTIONS whose prices derive from the UNDERLYING INSTRUMENT (for example shares or commodities etc).

devaluation   The reduction in value of a currency with respect to another.

devise [UK]   A FREEHOLD property given as a gift in a WILL.

diluted net asset value   A method of calculating the net asset value of a company, for example an investment trust, after taking into consideration any outstanding CONVERTIBLE LOAN STOCK, WARRANTS or OPTIONS which are assumed to be exercised by the holders, so increasing the number of shares among which the assets are divided.

Diners Club   An international CHARGE CARD enabling the holder to obtain goods and services without the need to pay cash. Invoices of transactions are tendered monthly which must be settled in full. There is no preset spending limit.

direct debit   A payment system in which the payer agrees to the payee (for example an insurance company) regularly taking funds from his/her specified bank account. This could typically be for monthly premiums for an insurance policy or for gas bills etc. If the payee needs to increase the regular amount, the customer must be informed prior to claiming the additional funds. See standing order.

direct purchase [USA]   The purchase of shares in an OPEN END MUTUAL FUND directly from the fund company rather than through a broker.

direct taxation   Taxes which are imposed directly on the individual paying them. Examples of direct taxation are INCOME TAX, CAPITAL GAINS TAX and ESTATE TAX (INHERITANCE TAX in the UK). See also indirect taxation.

disability income insurance [USA]   Insurance which provides an income to the policyholder when he/she is unable to work due to an illness or injury. Disability payments to insured persons, which normally commence after a set period (the ELIMINATION PERIOD), are usually tax free provided the premium payments are up to date.

disclosure [USA]   The providing of all relevant information by a company, which could influence investment decisions, this in accordance with the requirements of the SECURITIES AND EXCHANGE COMMISSION.

discount   1. The difference between the face value and the market price of a security.   **2. [UK]** A term used by INVESTMENT TRUSTS which refers to the difference between the NET ASSET VALUE per share and the share price expressed as a percentage of the net asset value per share, this being relevant whenever the share price is lower.   Under these circumstances the shares are said to trade at a discount.   When the share price is above the net asset value, it is said to trade at a PREMIUM.

discount rate [USA]   The interest rate at which the US FEDERAL RESERVE lends money to member banks.

discount yield [USA]   The yield on a security purchased at a price below its face value.

discretionary account   An account in which an investor authorises his/her stockbroker to make purchases and sales of securities on an ongoing basis without reference or approval.

discretionary trust   1. A trust that enables the trustees to use their discretion in relation to the distribution of funds to beneficiaries.   **2. [USA]**   A MUTUAL FUND where investments are made in a variety of differing securities depending on the decisions of the fund's management.

disposable income   The net amount of money available for spending from an individual's income after taxes and other deductions have been made.

distribution   1. The control of the sale of a large block of stock so as not to cause a fall in the price.   **2.** The payment of a DIVIDEND by a company out of its profits.

distribution period   The period following the dividend DECLARATION DATE to the DATE OF RECORD during which a stockholder must officially own shares to be entitled to the dividend.

diversification   The placing of investments over a range of financial products to reduce risk.

dividend   The DISTRIBUTION of part of a company's earnings to shareholders.   This is usually in the form of cash but can also be in the form of stock (stock dividend).   In the UK this is called a scrip dividend.

dividend cover   See cover.

dividend growth   The amount by which a company's yearly dividends grow compared with the previous year.

dividend payout ratio [USA]   The dividend paid by a company expressed as a percentage of earnings.
For example:
Earnings = $1,500,000   Dividend = $300,000.
Dividend payout ratio = $300,000/$1,500,000 = 20%.

dividend reinvestment   The reinvestment of dividends to purchase further shares in the company.

dividend yield   A company's dividend per share payment divided by the current share price.

dollar cost averaging [USA]   A plan which enables investors to accumulate shares in stock or a MUTUAL FUND by purchasing on a regular basis (for example monthly) with a fixed dollar amount. When the price is low, more shares will be purchased and fewer when the price is high. Also known as constant dollar plan. Known as pound cost averaging in the UK.

domicile   The country in which a person permanently resides and in which it is the intention to remain.

double indemnity   A term normally associated with accident insurance. Under certain conditions, for example a road accident, a policy will pay twice the normal sum to the insured.

double taxation   Taxation of corporate earnings and subsequently taxation of dividends.

double taxation relief   Persons resident and domiciled in the UK are liable to INCOME TAX from their worldwide income payable to the INLAND REVENUE. Other countries operate similar taxation rules so that there could arise a situation where an individual is subjected to double taxation. Double taxation relief can be obtained when agreements exist between countries whereby tax already paid on income in a foreign country is offset against the same tax liability in the home country or vice versa.

Dow Jones Industrial Average   The main USA share index which monitors the movement of 30 particular industrial companies traded on the NEW YORK STOCK EXCHANGE.

draft   An order in writing by one party to another party to pay a specified sum to a third party or bearer on a particular date. The party making the order or drawing the draft is known as the drawer. The party to whom the bill is addressed is the drawee (for example a bank). The party to whom the bill is payable is the payee.

dual capital trust   See split capital trust.

dual purpose fund [USA]   A closed end fund with a limited life and two main classes of shares. Holders of preferred shares receive all the income. Common shareholders receive all the fund's assets at expiry after preferred shareholders have been paid their fixed redemption price. Similar to a SPLIT CAPITAL INVESTMENT TRUST in the UK.

durable power of attorney [USA]   A POWER OF ATTORNEY which, subject to conditions and safeguards, continues in force even after the maker of the durable power of attorney (the principal) may become mentally incapable of conducting his/her affairs. Equivalent to enduring power of attorney in the UK.

E

each way [USA] Commission earned by a broker on both the sale and purchase of a trade.

early retirement For company pension schemes, an employee may retire at an early age provided it is authorised by the company. In the UK, qualifying ages are 50 for men and 45 for women. However, the amount of pension payable will reduce compared with the amount payable at NORMAL RETIREMENT AGE.

early withdrawal penalty A charge imposed on holders of fixed term investments in the event of withdrawal prior to maturity.

earned income Income such as a person's salary or wages. This is so classified since he/she has, in return, completed a job of work. This compares with such income as bank interest and company DIVIDENDS etc which are classed as UNEARNED INCOME. Income from pensions is also classified as earned income.

earned income credit [USA] A tax credit for persons with at least one child living in residence for over six months and income below a certain level.

earnest money [USA] A deposit given to a seller by the buyer in order to demonstrate good faith and ability to complete the transaction. In the event that the buyer fails to complete the sale, the earnest money will normally be forfeited.

earning asset Any asset which produces income.

earnings The annual profits of a company after deduction of tax, dividends to preferred stockholders (preference shareholders in the UK) and bondholders.

earnings cap [UK] **1.** A term which relates to a person's FINAL SALARY in an OCCUPATIONAL PENSION SCHEME taken out on or after 1st June 1989 (or 14th March 1989 if the scheme was new at that time) and is the upper limit of earnings allowable under the scheme. **2.** The upper limit of NET RELEVANT EARNINGS, qualifying for tax relief in a PERSONAL PENSION PLAN which in turn limits contributions.

earnings per share (EPS)   The EARNINGS of a company divided by the number of shares of common stock (ordinary shares in the UK).

earnings report   See profit and loss statement.

economics   The study of manufacturing, distribution and consumption of products and services in an economy.   This is broadly divided into macroeconomics and microeconomics. *Macroeconomics*: The study of a country's economy using such elements as unemployment, price levels, government spending, interest rates, national productivity etc and the influence of government policy on them. *Microeconomics:* The study of economic elements at the level of the household or the company. Persons within a household are primarily concerned with employment prospects and how taxation affects their income. Companies are mainly concerned with product costs and operating expenses etc.

effective tax rate [USA]   The ratio of tax paid in a tax year to the taxable income. For example:
$$\text{tax paid} = \$20{,}000 \quad \text{taxable pay} = \$75{,}000$$
$$\text{effective tax rate} = \$20{,}000/\$75{,}000 = 26.7\%$$

electronic funds transfer system (EFTS)   An electronic payment system in which a plastic card is used to purchase goods or services. Subsequently the seller obtains payment by the electronic transfer of funds from the purchaser's card account. Equivalent to electronic funds transfer at point of sale in the UK.

elimination period [USA]   The period, prior to payments to a policyholder by the insurers after a claim, during which no payments are made. Also known as waiting period. Known as deferment period in the UK.

emergency fund   Cash set aside in a dedicated interest account to cover unanticipated emergencies such as property repairs, medical expenses and auto repairs.

Employee Retirement Income Security Act (ERISA) [USA]   A federal law introduced for the protection of participants in private pension plans.

employee stock ownership plan (ESOP) [USA]   A plan devised to encourage employees to purchase stock in their company usually at a price below the market price.

emergency tax [UK]   A special coding used by employers when an employee's tax code is unknown. Individuals allocated this code will only receive a single person's allowance and as such may pay excessive tax (it is possible to pay insufficient tax under the emergency code). However this is corrected with a refund once the correct code becomes known and applied.

emerging markets   Markets which are not usually associated with traditional areas of investment. However, as their potential starts to become recognised they are seen as prospective growth areas although at higher risk.

emoluments   Total remuneration of an employee or director which includes salary and bonuses etc.

endowment [USA]   A gift such as money or property to an institution for a given purpose.

endowment assurance [UK]   A fixed term LIFE ASSURANCE policy in which provision is made for premiums to pay for life cover plus a savings/ investment element. The policy pays out a sum of money (the SUM ASSURED) on the death of the LIFE ASSURED or at a specified date (the maturity date) if the life assured survives the term. If an endowment policy is encashed in its early years any proceeds returnable to the policyholder will normally be below the value of the premiums paid up to cancellation.

endowment insurance [USA]   A CASH VALUE LIFE INSURANCE policy with a fixed term. Premiums are applied to give life insurance cover for the face amount and at the end of the term the cash value will equate to the face amount and be payable.

endowment mortgage [UK]   An INTEREST ONLY MORTGAGE which is ultimately repaid by the proceeds of an ENDOWMENT ASSURANCE policy which is assigned to the BUILDING SOCIETY providing the mortgage. The policyholder pays the building society interest only, for the term of the mortgage. The sum assured, which is payable on maturity or prior death of the policyholder is used to repay the mortgage. Policies are usually WITH PROFITS (or LOW COST ENDOWMENT), UNIT LINKED or UNITISED WITH PROFITS and sometimes this provides some additional capital for the policyholder after the building society has been repaid.

enduring power of attorney [UK]   A POWER OF ATTORNEY which, subject to conditions and safeguards continues in force even after the maker of the enduring power of attorney (the 'donor') may become mentally incapable of conducting his/her affairs. Equivalent to durable power of attorney in the USA.

enterprise zone [UK]   A region in which companies are encouraged by the government via tax advantages to set up business.

enterprise zone trust   A property trust which invests in ENTERPRISE ZONES.

equitable owner   The BENEFICIARY designated to receive property held in trust.

equities   Another name for the COMMON STOCK or ORDINARY SHARES of companies.

equity   The money value of an asset after deduction of debts. For example the owner of an asset valued at $8,000 who has still to repay $3,000 to a bank in conjunction with the purchase of the asset, is said to have an equity of $5,000 in the asset. The term also applies to the remaining assets in a company after all creditors have been paid.

equity options [UK]   OPTIONS on the shares of companies. Equity options are traded in the UK at the LONDON INTERNATIONAL FINANCIAL FUTURES AND OPTIONS EXCHANGE (LIFFE) and the LONDON SECURITIES AND DERIVATIVES EXCHANGE (OMLX).

ERNIE [UK]   An abbreviation for Electronic Random Number Indicator Equipment which selects the prizes in the premium bonds monthly draw. See under National Savings, premium bonds.

escalating annuity   See annuity.

estate   The total value of a deceased person's assets. For example:
Total value of property , automobile and all other possessions = $500,000.
Allowable deductions such as mortgage, overdraft at bank, credit cards and
   other expenses   = $ 70,000.
Total net value of estate   = $430,000.

estate agent   An agent who acts in the arrangements of property sales and purchases in return for a commission based on the selling price and payable by the seller.

estate duty [UK]   A former tax on a deceased person's estate and the forerunner of CAPITAL TRANSFER TAX which itself has been superseded by INHERITANCE TAX.

estate tax [USA]   A tax imposed by the federal government or state on the net value of a deceased person's estate after deduction of an EXCLU-SION. The net proceeds, after estate tax has been paid, pass to the beneficiaries. If the sole BENEFICIARY is a spouse, no tax is payable.

estimated tax [USA]   The estimated amount of tax owed for the forthcoming year less tax credits. A taxpayer will usually be required to pay 90% of this amount by way of WITHHOLDING and quarterly payments or 100% (minimum) of the previous year's tax.

euro   The successor to the EUROPEAN CURRENCY UNIT (ECU) as the European currency. The euro was introduced in 11 member states on 1st January 1999. They were Austria, Belgium, Finland, France, Germany, Ireland, Italy, Luxembourg, Netherlands, Portugal and Spain.

eurobond   A bond, issued and underwritten by international syndicates of banks and issuing houses and sold to investors (such as multinational corporations) outside the country in whose currency it is denominated. A eurobond is normally payable to the bearer and is free of tax.

eurocheque scheme   A European payment scheme in which a person may purchase goods and obtain cash in the local currency of a European country outside of his/her country of residence by way of eurocheques and a guarantee card and where the EC sign is displayed. The eurocheque is debited from the person's current account after currency conversion.

eurocurrency   A currency which is deposited in banks outside its country of origin. For example the eurodollar, eurodeutschmark and eurosterling.

eurodollar   US dollar currency deposited in banks outside the USA.

euromarkets   The markets in which EUROCURRENCIES are traded, the largest being London.

European Community (EC)   The current community (comprising Austria, Belgium, Denmark, Finland, France, Germany, Greece, Ireland, Italy, Luxembourg, Netherlands, Portugal, Spain, Sweden and United Kingdom (UK).

european currency unit (ECU)   A weighted average of European Community currencies with weighting tending to be proportional to a country's economy. The ecu has been superseded by the euro.

European Economic Community (EEC) The original economic community set up in 1957 by the 6 founder members (France, West Germany, Belgium, Luxembourg, Holland and Italy) and more commonly known as the Common Market. The Community is currently known as the EUROPEAN COMMUNITY.

European Free Trade Association (EFTA) An association of countries (originally comprising Denmark, United Kingdom, Austria, Switzerland, Portugal and Sweden), formed in 1960 mainly to abolish trade barriers between members.

European Monetary System (EMS) The monetary system of the EC which attempts to reduce the currency variations between members.

European style exercise An OPTION which may only be exercised by the holder at expiry. See also American Style Exercise.

ex Another word for 'without'. See ex all, ex dividend, ex rights and ex scrip (UK).

ex all Purchase of a security without entitlement to current DIVIDENDS, RIGHTS ISSUES or SCRIP ISSUES. This entitlement remains with the seller of the security.

ex dividend Purchase of a security without entitlement to current DIVIDENDS. This entitlement remains with the seller of the security.

ex gratia A payment made out of a sense of moral obligation. The payer however is not legally bound to do so.

ex rights Purchase of a security without entitlement to current RIGHTS ISSUES. This entitlement remains with the seller of the security.

ex scrip [UK] Purchase of a security without entitlement to current SCRIP ISSUES. This entitlement remains with the seller of the security.

exceptional items Costs which affect a company's profit (or loss) which are associated with normal activities but are exceptional in magnitude. See extraordinary items.

excess [UK] The specified amount a policyholder must bear before the insurers pay a CLAIM. The inclusion of an excess whether compulsory or voluntary or both lowers the premium.

Exchange Rate Mechanism (ERM)   The mechanism by which members of the EC formerly operated their currency exchange rates within given upper and lower limits. In January 1999 certain members of the EC adopted the EURO for their currency.

excise duty [UK]   A tax imposed on certain types of products including alcohol and tobacco which are produced in the UK. Customs duties apply to products imported to the UK.

excise taxes [USA]   Federal and state taxes on the sale or production of certain types of products such as alcohol and tobacco.

exclusion [USA]   1. A clause in an insurance policy which specifies items or conditions not covered. **2.** An item which is excluded from taxation such as contributions to an INDIVIDUAL RETIREMENT ACCOUNT.

execution only account   An account where a broker only carries out the instructions of the client and offers no advice.

executive insurance [USA] An insurance policy taken out on the life of a company executive or senior employee whose death would cause significant loss to the company. In the event of such a death the proceeds would be payable to the company. Known as keyman insurance in the UK.

executive pension plan   A pension plan which is tailored for directors and senior executive staff.

executor   A person appointed in a WILL to ensure that the wishes of the deceased are duly carried out.

executrix The feminine form of executor.

exemption [USA] An allowable expense subtracted from gross income to reduce income tax liability. An exemption can be classified as either personal or dependency and these are further subdivided into exemptions for: individual taxpayers; elderly and disabled taxpayers; dependent children and other dependants more than half of whose support is provided; total or partial blindness; a taxpayer's spouse.

exercise   When an OPTION holder takes up his/her option to buy/sell the UNDERLYING INSTRUMENT (for example shares, commodities etc) he/she is said to exercise it.

exercise notice   A formal notice from an OPTION HOLDER to an option WRITER that he/she wishes to buy/sell the UNDERLYING INSTRUMENT (for example, shares, commodities etc) at the EXERCISE PRICE.

exercise price   **1.** The price at which an OPTION holder can buy or sell the UNDERLYING INSTRUMENT (for example, shares, commodities etc). Also known as strike price. **2.** The price which a WARRANT holder must pay for the ordinary shares of a company when the warrants are exercised.

exit charge [UK]   Instead of making an INITIAL CHARGE, some UNIT TRUST companies (particularly PEP managers) make a charge if units are cashed in, for example, within five years. In the USA this is known as a back end load.

expenses in employment   If an employee incurs expenses wholly on behalf of his/her company which are not reimbursed, such expenses can be offset against tax. Examples are accommodation, meals and fees to professional organisations.

expiry date   **1.** The last day on which an OPTION can be traded (AMERICAN STYLE EXERCISE). **2.** The only day an option can be traded (EUROPEAN STYLE EXERCISE).

extended coverage   Insurance which extends the term of a warranty, typically covering repairs on appliances and cars, the premium usually being a one off payment.

extra dividend   A dividend paid additionally to the normal dividend when profits of a company are particularly high.

extraordinary items   Costs which affect a company's profit (or loss) which are not associated with normal activities and which are not expected to recur. See exceptional items.

extrinsic value   See time value.

F

face amount (face value) **1.** The value of a bond, note or other security as printed on the document. Throughout the life of a security, its price (market value) will fluctuate but at maturity the face amount is payable. **2.** The value denominated on a coin, banknote or stamp etc

fair value The price at which a FUTURES CONTRACT should trade to be equivalent to the purchase price of the UNDERLYING INSTRUMENT. In options trading the term is also used when referring to INTRINSIC VALUE.

fair market value The traded value of an asset agreed by seller and buyer.

fallen angel [USA] A bond which was issued at a rating of AAA to BBB (investment grade) which has since fallen in rating to BB or below. **[UK]** A once highly esteemed company which has undergone a down grading.

family income benefit (family income assurance) [UK] A type of TERM ASSURANCE in which, following the death of the LIFE ASSURED, instalments, rather than a lump sum, are paid to the BENEFICIARY for the remainder of the policy term. If the life assured lives to the end of the term, no benefit is payable.

Fannie Mae See Federal National Mortgage Association.

fat cat An individual able to create additional wealth from the investment of existing substantial assets. In the UK the term also refers to executives who have earned high salaries and bonuses on the performance of privatised companies and other organisations etc.

federal agency security [USA] A debt instrument with a high level of safety issued by a federal agency.

Federal Deposit Insurance Corporation (FDIC) [USA] The federal agency that acts as guarantor for funds deposited in member banks.

federal gift tax [USA] A federal tax levied on gifted property, money or securities. The tax is payable by the donor and based on FAIR MARKET

VALUE of the gift. A parent or parents making gifts to children are allowed to make transfers up to a specified amount without paying tax.

Federal Insurance Contributions Act (FICA) [USA]   The federal law which directs employers to withold a proportion of employees' salaries for payment to the government in order to provide future pension and other social security benefits.

Federal National Mortgage Association (FNMA) [USA]   A government backed corporation which purchases mortgages from lenders and resells them to investors. It is financed by the issue of debt securities. Equity shares, known as Fannie Maes, are traded on the NEW YORK STOCK EXCHANGE.

Federal Reserve System [USA]   The American central banking system which comprises 12 regional Federal Reserve Banks, their branches and all national and state banks within the system. The Federal Reserve sets monetary policy in the USA and regulates the banking system.

Fedwire [USA]   A computerized high speed communication system linking the banks within the FEDERAL RESERVE SYSTEM. The network enables transfers to be conducted at high speed for inter-bank dealings and customer transfers.

fiduciary   A person entrusted to manage the assets and interests of another. For example, an EXECUTOR in a will would be so described.

final dividend   The end of year dividend. In the UK, companies normally pay dividends twice per year, an interim and a final dividend, the latter normally being the larger of the two and being declared at the ANNUAL GENERAL MEETING. See dividend.

final salary [UK]   The basis of determining a person's pension entitlement in a FINAL SALARY SCHEME and which normally refers to an OCCUPATIONAL PENSION. Final salary is defined as either: 1. the total EMOLUMENTS in a year, in any of the five years immediately preceding retirement or 2. the average of total emoluments for periods of three consecutive years or more ending within ten years of retirement. (Directors who own 20% or more of a company's share capital must define their final salary according to 2. above). For persons joining a scheme on or after 1st June 1989 (or 14th March 1989 if the scheme was new at that time) an EARNINGS CAP will apply which limits the final salary to be used for calculating benefits.

final salary scheme (defined benefit scheme) A PENSION scheme in which an employee's pension is based on his/her number of years service and FINAL SALARY with each employer. In this type of scheme employees are typically provided with 1/60 of final salary for each year of service up to a maximum of 40/60 that is, two thirds of final salary. At retirement a tax free lump sum may be taken at the expense of a reduced pension.

finance house A company whose main purpose is the financing of hire purchase transactions.

financial adviser A professional person qualified to give advice to clients regarding investments such as life insurance, pensions, mutual funds/unit trusts and taxation etc. A financial adviser may charge a fee and/or receive a commission on a product recommended. In the UK a financial adviser is either independent that is, AN INDEPENDENT FINANCIAL ADVISER (IFA), or a COMPANY REPRESENTATIVE (tied agent). An independent financial adviser is free to recommend products from a number of companies and his/her selection will be based on which company and product would best suit the needs of the client. A company representative is authorised to recommend only the products of the company he/she represents.

financial futures FUTURES CONTRACTS where the UNDERLYING INSTRUMENTS are financial such as shares, interest rates, currencies and indexes etc.

financial institution An institution which accepts funds from the public and reinvests in bank deposits, bonds and stocks etc. These include banks and insurance companies. In the UK a BUILDING SOCIETY would be included.

financial intermediary An institution such as a bank, that accepts funds from various   sources and redistributes such funds to other parties whilst making its profit. Basically an intermediary is a go between for those who possess surplus money wishing to earn interest and those who require short or long term loans who will pay a higher rate of interest than those depositing.

financial pager A pocket sized pager with datascreen which can display a variety of financial information including equities, bonds, futures and market news etc plus facilities for alert for limit breaches. The type of information transmitted is dependent on the service provider.

financial planner A professional person qualified to give clients a FINANCIAL PLANNING service.

financial planning   A service provided by a financial planner. This is a long term service provided for clients which considers all their financial affairs and which develops a plan for their financial objectives to be achieved. The plan is regularly reviewed to ensure goals remain on target with modifications being made as necessary.

Financial Services Act 1986 [UK]   A Government Act introduced primarily to provide increased protection for investors and to regulate investment business conducted in the UK.

Financial Services Authority (FSA) [UK]   The replacement regulating body for the Securities and Investments Board (SIB). The FSA, which came into being on 28th October 1997, carries all regulatory responsibilities for the UK financial services industry. The overall broad objectives are the protection of consumers of financial services, the promotion of clean and orderly markets and the maintenance of confidence in the financial services system. It is a criminal offence to conduct investment business without authorisation and the FSA is empowered to prosecute those who break this rule. A CENTRAL REGISTER is held which lists firms with authorisation.

financial statement   A statement which lists a balance sheet (depicting assets, liabilities and capital), income statement, cash flow statement and net worth.

Financial Times Indices [UK]   A wide range of indices including shares, stocks and fixed interest securities published by the Financial Times. The indices serve as indicators of trends of prices on the LONDON STOCK EXCHANGE and foreign exchanges. See FT-A All Share Index, FT-SE-A 350 Index, FT-SE 100 Index (Footsie) etc.

first mortgage   A mortgage which carries priority over any subsequent SECOND MORTGAGE. In the event of default, the lender (mortgagee) providing the first mortgage will receive precedence.

fiscal policy   The use of spending and taxation by the government in order to achieve its economic objectives. See monetary policy.

fiscal year   The tax year commencing 1st July. In the UK the fiscal year commences on 6th April.

fixed annuity [USA]   An ANNUITY which guarantees payments to an annuitant which are fixed for life or a specific period. Similar to a level annuity in the UK.

fixed assets Assets of a company such as buildings and machinery which are regularly used over a long period of time for the purpose of generating profits.

fixed income securities Securities such as government, municipal and corporate bonds which pay a fixed rate of interest until maturity. Also PREFERRED STOCK where fixed payments are referred to as dividends.

fixed rate mortgage A type of MORTGAGE where interest repayments to the lender are fixed until maturity or for a specified term.

flat yield The return (interest) on a FIXED INTEREST SECURITY expressed as a percentage of its current market price. See also bond yield.

flexible pension [UK] Also known as deferred income and income drawdown. See personal pension plan.

flotation The establishment of a public company by an OFFER FOR SALE of shares to the public or by a PLACING. This enables the company to raise capital for its future growth. Known as an INITIAL PUBLIC OFFERING (IPO) in the USA.

footsie The Financial Times 100 Share Index (FTSE 100 Index).

foreclosure The procedure by which a homeowner forfeits his/her property to the lender (mortgagee) following default. This could be failure to pay interest on the loan. A foreclosure order is given by a court.

force majeure Unforeseeable events, beyond the control of participants in a contract, which may excuse either side from fulfilling its liabilities.

foreign exchange Currencies issued by foreign countries.

forward dealing The buying or selling of UNDERLYING INSTRUMENTS such as COMMODITIES, securities and currencies etc for delivery at a specified future date and a fixed price.

forward pricing The setting of the price (which then remains fixed) for FORWARD DEALING. This occurs at the time the contract is established.

fourth market [USA] The market of securities trading without the participation of brokers, thus obviating commission costs. The market, which is computer based, mainly comprises large institutional investors such as mutual funds and insurance companies.

franchise   A licence, granted by one company (franchisor) to another company or person (franchisee/licence holder), entitling the licence holder to produce or market a product in a specific area. The licence is usually reviewed periodically, typically every 6 months or annually.

franchisee   See franchise.

franchisor   See franchise.

franked income [UK]   Dividends, paid by UK companies to other companies (for example, investment trusts), with a tax credit reflecting the fact that the company which has paid the dividend has done so out of post tax profits. Therefore the 'franked income' will be free of further tax to the receiving company.

free standing additional voluntary contributions (FSAVC) [UK]   An employee's pension scheme which is additional to but independent from his/her OCCUPATIONAL PENSION SCHEME. The maximum amount which may currently be contributed to an employee's pension funds is 15% of remuneration (which includes benefits in kind) including his/her company scheme. For example if an employee is in a company scheme into which he/she contributes 10% of remuneration, a further 5% may be additionally paid by that employee in a tax year into FSAVCs or AVCs. However, the employer and employee contributions when combined must not produce benefits in excess of INLAND REVENUE maximums.

freehold [UK]   The permanent ownership of land or buildings which can be legally passed on to heirs and the most usual form of ownership for houses. Also known as property that is held in 'fee simple'.

Friendly Societies Commission [UK]   The current regulator of friendly societies in the UK. Regulation is expected to pass to the FINANCIAL SERVICES AUTHORITY (FSA) during the latter part of 1999.

friendly society [UK]   A MUTUAL ORGANISATION whose funds, after the deduction of running costs, are owned by its policyholders. The main purpose of a friendly society is to provide life assurance and to assist members during sickness and unemployment. They were first formed around the sixteenth century in order to provide protection for the families of working individuals in the event of their death or illness and to encourage self reliance. Some of these societies grew into large mutual insurance companies and still exist today. Friendly societies are currently regulated by the FRIENDLY SOCIETIES COMMISSION although future responsibility will pass to the FINANCIAL SERVICES AUTHORITY (FSA).

Where societies advertise and market life assurance products, they are regulated by the PERSONAL INVESTMENT AUTHORITY (PIA).

fringe benefits   Benefits to employees additional to salary. Typical examples would be company cars, expense accounts and private medical insurance which in the USA are not normally taxable. However they would be liable for tax in the UK.

front end load   A charge imposed by a management company on a MUTUAL FUND or UNIT TRUST to cover administration costs and commission at the time of purchase.

FTSE All Share Index   The Financial Times' publication of an overall index of the share prices of over 800 leading companies on the London Stock Exchange from all sectors and a reflection of the general trend of the market. The performance of funds under management are often compared with this index. See below examples of other Financial Times' Indices.

FTSE 350 Index   A combined index of the FTSE 100 and the FTSE 250.

FTSE 100 Index (Footsie)   An index of the share prices of the 100 largest companies (by MARKET CAPITALISATION) in the UK which is constantly updated. The index was started in 1984 with a base of 1,000.

FTSE 250 Index   An index of the share prices of the 250 largest companies (by MARKET CAPITALISATION) immediately following the largest 100 (FT-SE 100).

FT Ordinary Share Index (FT 30 Index)   An index of the share prices of 30 leading companies in the UK selected to depict British Industry.

FT Government Securities   An index of a range of Government Securities (gilts) prices.

FT Eurotop 300   An index of the share prices of the 300 largest European companies (by MARKET CAPITALISATION).

full disclosure   The obligation to disclose all factual information relevant to a contract.

full endowment [UK]   An ENDOWMENT policy in which the savings element is significantly increased.

full faith and credit [USA]   Effectively a guarantee of payment of interest and repayment of principal of a bond issued by a government authority.

full structural   An extensive property survey.

fully invested   When all money in a portfolio is invested in securities as opposed to retaining some cash, it is said to be fully invested.

fully paid policy   A LIFE INSURANCE policy which remains in force where the INSURED has paid premiums over part of the term of the policy but is unable to make further payments. In these circumstances the cash or surrender value is used to purchase a single premium policy which pays a reduced amount either on the death of the insured or on maturity if a term is specified other than life.

fund   A pool of money normally set apart for a purpose, for example, a pension fund to provide pensions.

fund switching   The movement of assets in one MUTUAL FUND or UNIT TRUST to another within a range of funds with differing objectives, all managed by the same investment company

fund value   The monetary value of a FUND.

fundamental analysis   The analysis of a company's financial statement so as to forecast future growth prospects and assess whether the current share price is properly valued.

further advance   The raising of capital by a mortgagor (borrower) from his/her existing mortgagee (lender). This could occur when for example both the value of the property and the mortgagor's salary has increased over the years. Under these circumstances the existing lender may consider the advancing of further capital to the mortgagor provided he/she can afford the higher repayments. The interest rate will not necessarily be the same as the existing rate but usually similar.

futures   See futures contract.

futures contract   A legal agreement to make or take delivery of a specified instrument (for example, a commodity such as coffee or a financial instrument such as shares) at a fixed future date at a price determined at the time of dealing.

G

gain   The difference between the selling price and purchase price of a SECURITY. See capital gains tax.

gamma shares [UK]   A term previously given to the shares of smaller companies traded far less frequently on the LONDON STOCK EXCHANGE than alpha and beta shares. These terms were replaced by the NORMAL MARKET SIZE classification in January 1991.

garnishee   The recipient (typically a bank) to whom a GARNISHEE ORDER has been delivered.

garnishee order [UK]   A court order instructing a garnishee (a bank) that funds held on behalf of a debtor (the judgement debtor) should not be released until directed by the court. The order may also instruct the bank to pay a given sum to the judgement creditor (the person to whom a debt is owed by the judgement debtor) from these funds.

garnishment [USA]   A court order instructing an employer to withhold all or part of an employee's salary and to submit this amount (and subsequent amounts if relevant) to the court for settlement of a debt or other legal obligation to another party.

gearing [UK]   **1.** The capital structure of a company which is the ratio of its debt (loan capital such as debentures etc) to its equity capital (ordinary share capital plus retained profits). The American term for gearing is LEVERAGE. Where a company is financed largely by loan capital rather than by equity capital, it is said to be highly geared. **2.** A term which refers to borrowings by an INVESTMENT TRUST which boost the return on capital and income via additional investment. When the trust is performing well shareholders enjoy an enhanced or geared profit. However if the trust performs poorly then the loss is similarly exaggerated. **3.** A term used in WARRANTS which refers to the ratio between a company's share price and its warrant price.

General Agreement on Tariffs and Trade (GATT)   A trade agreement between a large number of countries, dating back to 1948, which was set up to improve trading world wide and to work towards the reduction of tariff barriers.

---

general lien   The legal right for a CREDITOR to seize the assets of a DEBTOR to satisfy an outstanding debt.

general obligation bond [USA]   A municipal bond whose interest and principal payments are supported by the FULL FAITH AND CREDIT of the issuing authority.

general personal equity plan   See personal equity plan.

gift   A transfer of an asset such as property or money etc from one person to another where no payment of any kind is given by the receiving person to the donor. Transfers of this kind may be subject to inheritance tax if the value is above a certain amount and to capital gains tax in certain circumstances.

gifts to charity   See single gifts to charity.

gift tax [USA]   A tax imposed by the federal government or state on the donor of a gift when the transfer of money or property passes from one individual to another. A parent or parents making gifts to children are allowed to make transfers up to a specified amount without paying tax. In the UK there is currently no gift tax in operation although there is a potential liability for INHERITANCE TAX when gifts are made. See potentially exempt transfer (PET).

gilt edged securities [USA]   Bonds of companies with a high reputation for dependency for the payment of bond interest. **[UK] (gilts)**   Fixed interest stocks issued by the British Government and called gilts because of the gilt edged surround on original certificates. These stocks (or securities) are traded on the LONDON STOCK EXCHANGE and their prices influenced by items such as interest rates and other market conditions. Gilts are normally issued in units of £100 and if they are (what are known as) REDEEMABLE, the £100 is repaid to whoever happens to be the owner at the REDEMPTION DATE. Redeemable gilts are classified as longs (redeemable after fifteen years or more), mediums (redeemable between five and fifteen years) and shorts (redeemable within five years). Income from gilts is liable for tax but all capital gains are tax free. In the USA the equivalent government debt instruments are TREASURY SECURITIES.

Gilt Edged Market Makers (GEMMs)   MARKET MAKERS dealing in gilts.

gilts   See gilt edged securities [UK].

Ginnie Mae   See Government National Mortgage Association (GNMA).

Girobank plc [UK]   Girobank was established in 1968 and known then as the National Girobank. It was set up by the Post Office and provided a public banking facility for people without bank accounts. An additional advantage was that the number of post offices around the country were greater than the number of banks. In modern times Girobank plc resembles the high street banks in the services provided.

global fund [USA]   A mutual fund which invests in securities in countries around the world such as Europe and Asia as well as the USA.

going long   See long position.

going short   See short position.

gold card   A plastic payment card which normally allows the holder higher spending limits over the standard card. Also loan facilities are sometimes available. Persons holding such a card are often required to be earning a minimum salary level. Gold cards are usually either CHARGE CARDS or CREDIT CARDS.

good till cancelled order   An order to a broker to buy or sell a security at a specified price which remains valid until cancelled by the client or by execution.

government securities   See gilt edged securities.

Government National Mortgage Association (GNMA) [USA]   A government owned corporation which guarantees payment of interest and principal of mortgage backed PASS THROUGH SECURITIES. The corporation is nicknamed Ginnie Mae.

grace period   The period, normally 30 days during which an insurance policy remains in force even though the premium has not been paid.

graduated payment mortgage (GPM) [USA]   A mortgage scheme in which monthly payments commence at a lower level and increase over a period of a few years to a higher level which is subsequently maintained.

Graduated Pension [UK]   See National Insurance (NI) Pension.

Graduated Retirement Benefit [UK]   See National Insurance (NI) Pension.

granny bonds [UK]   Index-linked savings certificates. They were originally introduced for people who were over retirement age.

grantee [UK]   A term, used by some assurance companies, as an alternative to ASSURED.

grant of probate   See probate.

gray knight [USA] grey knight [UK]   A company (or person), making an unwanted counter bid for another company, whose intentions are unclear. See black knight. See white knight.

gross   Before any deductions.

gross domestic product (GDP)   The value of all goods and services created within an economy over a specified time which is usually one year.

gross income [USA]   The total income of a person (salary, dividend and interest income, capital gains etc) before EXCLUSIONS and DEDUCTIONS. **[UK]**   The total income of a person prior to the subtraction of TAX ALLOWANCES. This for example could be a person's salary plus bonuses plus benefits in kind (company car and medical insurance) plus income from shares etc. See net income.

gross interest   **1.**   Interest earned by deposits at banks and financial institutions, also GILTS etc before deduction of tax. **2.**   Interest charged on bank loans etc before any tax relief is taken into account.

gross margin   The difference between the selling price of an item and the purchase or manufacturing cost, expressed as a percentage of the selling price. For example a company's manufacturing cost of an item is $6 and the selling price is $10. Gross margin = $[(\$10 - \$6)/\pounds 10] \times 100 = 40\%$.

gross national product (GNP)   The addition of GROSS DOMESTIC PRODUCT and various forms of income from abroad.

gross profit   **1.** The difference between the selling price of an item and the purchase or manufacturing cost. **2.** A company's total turnover of products sold less costs to purchase or manufacture. See net profit.

gross rate   **1.** The interest rate earned by deposits at banks and financial institutions before deduction of tax, for example, 5% gross rate. **2.** The interest rate charged on bank loans, and mortgage interest etc before any tax relief is taken into account.

gross redemption yield   See redemption yield.

gross yield The YIELD on a SECURITY before the deduction of tax.

grossing up The adjusting of a net return on an investment to the gross equivalent, that is adding back the tax deducted to obtain the gross return.

ground rent [UK] Rent payable by the owner of a LEASEHOLD PROPERTY to the FREEHOLD owner.

group insurance Insurance provided for company employees by employers. Items covered may include health insurance, disability insurance and term life insurance. It would be considerably more expensive for a single employee to obtain such insurance.

Group of Seven (G7) The seven foremost industrial countries outside what was the communist bloc. They are USA, Germany, Japan, United Kingdom, France, Canada and Italy. The main objectives are the discussions of economic and political issues of common interest to the group.

growth An asset which increases in value.

growth and income fund A MUTUAL FUND or UNIT TRUST which aims to provide investors with continuing dividend payments plus capital gains.

growth fund A MUTUAL FUND or UNIT TRUST which aims to provide investors with capital growth

growth bond A bond which gives capital growth at maturity.

growth stocks Stocks (shares) whose share values have grown at an above average rate over a number of years and which are expected to continue to grow at a high rate.

guarantee **1.** A commitment made by a person to be answerable for the debts or liabilities of another. **2. [UK]** A document, supplied by a manufacturer, indicating that in the event of product failure it will be repaired or replaced. This usually involves a specified time period. In the USA this is known as a warranty.

guaranteed death benefit [UK] A life policy in which there is a minimum sum payable on the death of the LIFE ASSURED.

guaranteed growth bond A bond in which a single premium secures a guaranteed amount at its maturity date.

guaranteed income bond   A bond in which a single premium secures a guaranteed regular income until maturity at which time the original premium is returned.

guaranteed minimum pension [UK]   The minimum pension payable by a pension scheme in order that members may contract out of SERPS.

guaranteed minimum period   The period during which an ANNUITY is paid irrespective of whether the ANNUITANT dies during that period. If the annuitant lives beyond this period, payments continue until death. An annuity with such a guarantee could benefit people, with dependants, who require the income to continue after their death. This means that the sum of money paid for the annuity would not be wasted in the event of early death.

guaranteed renewable policy   An insurance policy which is guaranteed renewable provided premiums are paid. The policy conditions remain unchanged although the insurers may review premium rates.

guaranteed sum assured [UK]   A term used by some life companies which refers to the minimum sum payable by a life policy either on the death of the LIFE ASSURED or on maturity.

guarantor   A person who commits to guarantee the debts of another. For example if an individual fails to meet his/her obligations on say hire purchase repayments, the guarantor will be obliged to make those repayments.

H

Hang Seng Index The main indicator of stock market performance in Hong Kong based on 33 companies. The index is arithmetically calculated and weighted by MARKET CAPITALISATION.

hard currency A currency which is generally accepted throughout the world and which is unlikely to devalue. Examples are the deutschmark, dollar and Swiss franc.

hard dollars [USA] Payment to a broker (excluding the earning of any commissions) by a customer for services provided. This payment could be for advice or for providing a financial plan.

health insurance [USA] Generic term for insurance covering costs incurred due to illness, injury and disability.

heavy market [USA] A market in which there are more sellers than buyers resulting in falling prices.

hedge ratio The number of FUTURES or OPTIONS contracts required to HEDGE/ counteract the exposure in the UNDERLYING INSTRUMENT (for example shares, commodities etc).

hedging (hedge) A strategy employed in a FUTURES market to reduce risk. This is achieved by establishing a position which is broadly opposite to that held in the UNDERLYING INSTRUMENT (for example shares, commodities etc).

Her Majesty's Customs and Excise [UK] The government department which collects customs and excise duties and VAT.

hidden values [USA] Assets owned by a company but undervalued on the balance sheet and accordingly not exhibited in the stock price. Similar to hidden reserve in the UK.

high current income fund [USA] A mutual fund which seeks to pay a high dividend to its shareholders. This may be by way of JUNK BONDS which pay higher levels of income but with the attendant higher risk.

---

high equity   A MORTGAGE which is low in comparison to the amount deposited in cash by the purchaser.

high grade security [USA]   A bond, issued by a highly regarded company or municipal authority with a rating of AAA or AA.

high-tech stocks   The stocks of companies participating in high technology fields such as computers, semiconductors and electronics.

higher rate adjustment [UK]   An INCOME TAX coding which is relevant to persons who pay tax at the higher rate. For interest received from banks or DIVIDENDS from shares etc, the higher rate adjustment enables the Inland Revenue to collect the additional tax due over and above the BASIC RATE. The additional tax can, if required, be paid separately.

higher rate tax [UK]   The highest rate of INCOME TAX in the UK which is immediately above the BASIC RATE.

hire purchase   A transaction in which the purchaser of goods pays an initial deposit and takes possession. Subsequent instalments are made over a specified time after which ownership passes to the purchaser.

historical volatility   See volatility.

holder   1. A person in possession of a NEGOTIABLE INSTRUMENT such as a BILL OF EXCHANGE or PROMISSORY NOTE. That person may be the payee or the endorsee. **2.** A person who has made an OPENING PURCHASE of an OPTION and thus has acquired the rights to them.

holder of record [USA]   The owner of securities whose name is registered by the issuing company or its TRANSFER AGENT as from a particular date.

holding company   A company which holds the majority of shares in its subsidiaries. Also known as the parent company.

holding period [USA]   The length of time an individual retains hold of an investment. If an investment is held for more than one year the capital gain liability is reduced. In the UK there is an annual capital gains tax (CGT) allowance after which a tapering of CGT applies. This allows a tapering reduction of tax rates over the longer term.

holiday insurance [UK]   A policy which covers the INSURED and usually his/her family for the duration of their holiday. Items covered normally include travel delays, unavoidable cancellation, baggage loss and damage, loss of personal items including cash and credit cards, personal accident and medical expenses abroad etc.

home banking   A facility provided by banks enabling customers to conduct banking transactions through their personal computer and telephone line link via a modem. This system allows instant access to bank balances and the provision for transferring funds.

home income plan [UK]   A plan enabling the normally elderly owner or owners of a property to utilise its capital value to his/her or their advantage (by providing an income) and still remain in residence. Typically a BUILDING SOCIETY or insurance company provides a loan of up to 80% of the property value and this loan is used to purchase an annuity or joint life annuity (see annuity) in the case of say joint owners. The annuity payments are used to pay interest on the loan and provided 90% of the loan is invested in this way tax relief can be claimed. (The remaining 10% of the loan can usually be taken in cash with no restrictions). Thus after making interest payments net of tax relief there will be a surplus available to the owner or owners. There may be some tax payable on the interest part of the annuity dependent on individual circumstances. On the death of the owner (or second of joint owners) the property is sold to repay the loan with any surplus passing to dependants.

home reversion plan [UK]   A plan which offers elderly persons the opportunity of raising cash on their property. A financial institution such as an insurance company makes a purchase at a price well below market value with the original owners being entitled to live in the property until their death. The cash received is used to purchase an annuity on which tax would be payable on the interest portion.

homeowners equity account   A credit line offered by banks and mortgage lenders which grants the homeowner the opportunity of borrowing against the built up equity in the property.

homeowners insurance [USA]   A form of property insurance which provides cover against such items as damage to the building, personal property, theft, personal liability etc.

hospital income policy [USA] hospital cash plan [UK]   An insurance policy which pays a specified amount to the insured in the event that he/she goes to hospital. This is usually to provide for lost income.

hostile takeover   A takeover bid by one company for another, the latter being opposed to such a bid.

house call [USA]   The notification to a client by a brokerage house that more funds are required to bring a MARGIN ACCOUNT balance up to the required level.

household insurance [UK]   Insurance covering the structure or contents of a house. This type of insurance now tends to include the option of cover for additional items such as legal expenses. Also some companies now offer no claims bonuses similar to those given by motor insurance companies. See buildings insurance and contents insurance.

I

identified shares [USA]   The shares of stock or a MUTUAL FUND carrying a record of purchase price and date of purchase. For example if shares are being accumulated through a CONSTANT DOLLAR PLAN there will be an ongoing record of all share purchase prices and purchase dates which enables the COST BASIS to be established. When shares are sold the owner can identify those which were purchased at higher prices in order to keep capital gains tax to a minimum.

IFA Association [UK]   An association formed in September 1994 by a merger of the National Federation of Independent Financial Advisers (NFIFA) and the financial services arm of the BRITISH INSURANCE AND INVESTMENT BROKERS ASSOCIATION (BIIBA). It formed the premier trade association to represent IFA firms irrespective of their size or how their business is obtained.

IFA Promotion [UK]   An organisation established in 1989 to improve the image of INDEPENDENT FINANCIAL ADVISERS (IFAs) and their work and to encourage consumers to seek independent financial advice. It is the largest representative body for IFAs in the UK with over 14,000 members in 8,500 companies and branches drawn from all regulatory bodies including the FINANCIAL SERVICES AUTHORITY (FSA), SELF REGULATING ORGANISATIONS (SROs) such as the PERSONAL INVESTMENT AUTHORITY (PIA) and RECOGNISED PROFESSIONAL BODIES (RPBs) such as the LAW SOCIETY and the INSTITUTE OF CHARTERED ACCOUNTANTS IN ENGLAND AND WALES (ICAEW).

immediate annuity   See annuity.

in house   A term used in banking which refers to settlement of payments between accounts both held at the same branch.

in the money   1. A call option with an EXERCISE PRICE below, or a PUT OPTION with an exercise price above the UNDERLYING INSTRUMENT (for example shares, commodities). They are said to have INTRINSIC VALUE. **2.** Warrants with an exercise price below the market price.

incapacity benefit [UK]   A state benefit payable after the expiry of state SICKNESS BENEFIT if a person is still unfit to work. This replaces the former

INVALIDITY BENEFIT and as such carries a reduced level of benefit. The number of persons who can qualify for this benefit has also reduced.

incentive stock option [USA]   A stock option, which specifies a set number of shares at a specified option price extending over a given period, which is free of tax when granted and when exercised. If the stock is subsequently sold two years or more after the grant date or one year or more after the transfer to an employee, a reduced capital gains tax liability on profits will apply.

income   1. Money received by an individual in return for his/her work effort that is salary or wages. **2.** Money received by an individual from investments, for example bank interest and share dividends.

income bond   A bond which provides income over its life and at maturity the original investment is returned. See guaranteed income bond.

income dividend [USA]   A distribution of interest or dividends to the shareholders of a MUTUAL FUND.

income drawdown [UK]   Also known as deferred income and flexible pension. See personal pension plan.

income endowment [UK]   An ENDOWMENT plan which carries an option at maturity for the proceeds to be paid in the form of a regular income.

income fund [USA]   A MUTUAL FUND whose aim is to provide shareholders with CURRENT INCOME.

income from property [UK]   Income received from property letting is subject to income tax. The amount taxable is the amount receivable in the tax year. If an owner occupier or tenant rents out a room he/she may receive up to a certain annual income without incurring a tax liability.

income limit for age related allowances [UK]   Persons aged 65 to 74 are entitled to an additional personal tax allowance provided total earnings do not exceed a given amount. This allowance is further increased for persons aged 75 and over. Also a married man, living with his wife where either person is over the age of 65, is entitled to an additional married couple's allowance provided his total earnings do not exceed that same given amount. In cases where total earnings exceed this figure, these allowances are reduced by £1 for every £2 of income earned above this amount

income pure endowment   An ENDOWMENT plan which carries an option at maturity for the proceeds to be paid in the form of a regular income. In the event of the policyholder's death before maturity no benefit is payable.

income shares   **1.** Shares purchased in anticipation of an above average income being produced. Also referred to as high YIELD shares. **2.** Those shares in a DUAL PURPOSE FUND (SPLIT CAPITAL INVESTMENT TRUST in the UK) which receive most or all of the trust's income. The other class of shares (capital shares) receive the fund's capital.

income stock [USA]   A reputable stock with a record of consistently high dividend payments to shareholders.

income tax [USA]   The taxation of income by the federal government, state and local governments. TAXABLE INCOME, on which tax liability is computed, is assessed by subtracting deductions and exemptions from gross income. There is a range of tax brackets and as taxable income increases from one bracket to another the tax rate increases.   **[UK]** The DIRECT TAXATION of a person's earned income (for example salary/wages) and unearned income (for example building society interest and share dividends). The tax is levied on GROSS INCOME less allowances and reliefs, this being known as taxable income.

income tax allowances   See tax allowances.

income tax schedules A, B, C, D, E, F.   See Taxation Schedules A, B, C, D, E, F.

increasing life annuity   Another expression for ESCALATING ANNUITY. See annuity.

increasing term assurance   See term assurance.

indemnity   An agreement in which one person is answerable for restoring the losses of another.

indemnity commission   Where a life company pays commission to an agent, the company does so on the proviso it will be entitled to take back some or all (CLAWBACK) such commission if the relevant policy is cancelled within a given period.

indemnity insurance   A policy which covers the INSURED against the loss of an asset or incurring a liability by reimbursement of money etc. The purpose of such insurance is to place the insured in exactly the same financial state after a loss as he/she was in before such loss occurred.

indenture [USA]   A written agreement (also called a deed of trust) between a bond issuer and a purchaser which details: description of bond; amount of the issue; property pledged if not a debenture; covenants; working capital and current ratio; redemption rights or privileges. A trustee also acts on behalf of all bondholders. **[UK]**   A written agreement between two persons. This term is used between a master and apprentice.

independent financial adviser (IFA)   See financial adviser.

index   A number which represents a set of data and which is measured on an ongoing basis with a view to tracking changes from a given base. For example in the USA the CONSUMER PRICE INDEX gives a measure of the change in the cost of living. The STANDARD AND POOR'S COMPOSITE INDEX (S&P 500) measures the share prices of 500 US companies and reflects the general trend of the US stock market. The FTSE 100 Index is a measure of the combined share prices of the 100 largest companies in the UK.

index fund   A fund which invests to perform in line with a stock exchange index such as the Standard and Poor's 500 Index and the FTSE 100 Index in the UK. Over the long term it is argued that very few fund managers outperform the index against which their funds are compared. Also because costs are kept to a minimum (no fees for active fund management), an investment in an index fund will purchase more shares or units than in a managed fund. Sometimes known as a tracker fund.

index linked   The coupling of such items as salaries and pensions etc to the RETAIL PRICE INDEX in order to take account of INFLATION.

index linked family income assurance [UK}   FAMILY INCOME ASSURANCE in which the ASSURED may, if he or she chooses, increase premiums in line with the RETAIL PRICE INDEX and hence increase the SUM ASSURED.

index linked term assurance [UK]   TERM ASSURANCE in which premiums are increased in line with the RETAIL PRICE INDEX and hence the SUM ASSURED is increased.

index options   Call or put options on an index such as the Standard and Poor's 500 Index or the FTSE 100 Index. Such options are exercisable into cash rather than the underlying shares as is the case with EQUITY

OPTIONS. In the USA, index options are traded on a number of exchanges including the New York and Chicago Board Options Exchanges. In the UK, index options are traded on the LONDON INTERNATIONAL FINANCIAL FUTURES AND OPTIONS EXCHANGE. (LIFFE)

indexation   The factor by which wages and pensions etc are multiplied in order to be linked to an index. This factor is intended to account for INFLATION. In the USA indexing wages to the CONSUMER PRICE INDEX (CPI) may apply. In the UK indexation of items such as wages and pensions to the RETAIL PRICE INDEX may be relevant. See indexation allowance.

indexation allowance [UK]   An allowance given against capital gains tax (CGT) which previously took into account increases in the values of assets (for example shares) due to INFLATION. Indexation was frozen as from 6th April 1998 and replaced by a tapering of CGT over time. See capital gains tax.

indirect taxation   Taxation which is paid to the government in an indirect way, for example in the UK, VALUE ADDED TAX (VAT) charged on goods and services. VAT is the main indirect tax in the UK and is ultimately paid by the consumer. However the consumer may be said to have the choice as to whether or not goods or services are purchased whereas DIRECT TAXATION is paid automatically when, for example, a person's income, capital gains or ESTATE values exceed a certain level.

individual retirement account (IRA) [USA]   A TAX DEFERRED retirement savings account which may be set up by persons in employment. Annual contributions are limited to $2,000 or $4,000 for a couple (£2,250 if one works and other earns an income below $250). IRA contributions are tax deductible irrespective of income if neither spouse is a member of a QUALIFIED PLAN OR TRUST. A person who *is* a member of a qualified plan may still deduct IRA contributions providing ADJUSTED GROSS INCOME is below a certain level. Although savings grow tax free over the term of the plan, when pension benefits are taken, they will be liable to tax.

individual savings account (ISA) [UK]   A tax favoured savings account introduced on 6th April 1999 which replaced PEPs and TESSAs. Persons over the age of 18 can invest a maximum of £5,000 per year in each tax year for a period of ten years with a review after seven years. In the first year from 6th April 1999 the limit will be £7,000. Investment may be made in equities or between EQUITIES, cash and LIFE ASSURANCE. For the first year up to £3,000 can be invested in cash and thereafter no more than £1,000 annually (hence the limit of £7,000 total in the first year). No more than £1,000 per year may be invested in life assurance.

For the first five years ISAs will benefit from a 10% tax credit on UK equities. Equities which can be held in an ISA include UNIT TRUSTS, OPEN ENDED INVESTMENT COMPANIES (OEICs), INVESTMENT TRUSTS, ORDINARY SHARES, PREFERENCE SHARES and fixed interest CORPORATE BONDS. PEPs in existence at 6th April 1999 may, if required be held outside an ISA with the same tax advantages. TESSAs in existance at 6th April 1999 are allowed to run their full five year term.

industrial life assurance [UK]   An ASSURANCE policy on the life of an individual where weekly or monthly premiums are regularly paid to the assurance company by way of their agent who collects directly from the policyholder's home. This method of collection originated in industrial areas as a means of saving for a future lump sum or protection against industrial accidents etc. This type of assurance is now virtually extinct.

inflation   The increasing of wages and prices in an economy over a period of time, usually annualised for comparative purposes.

inheritance tax [UK]   A tax charged on the assets of a deceased person's ESTATE after a tax free allowance is made. There is an additional charge on gifts over £3,000 in any year given within the 7 years preceding death which is made on a diminishing scale. See potentially exempt transfer (PET). The rate of inheritance tax payable is at the highest rate (currently 40%).

initial charge   A charge imposed by a management company on a UNIT TRUST to cover administration costs (also known as front end load).

initial margin [USA]   Payment required to be made by an investor to a broker to open a MARGIN ACCOUNT. Once initial margin is deposited the investor may deal on credit from the broker. The credit extended is directly related to the margin deposited which itself is dependent on the purchase price of a securities transaction. **[UK]** The returnable, initial outlay of money required from a FUTURES or OPTIONS trader as security against default.

initial public offering (IPO) [USA]   The first offering of a corporation's stock to the public. Known as a flotation in the UK.

Inland Revenue [UK]   The government department responsible to the Treasury for the collection of direct taxes which include INCOME TAX, CAPITAL GAINS TAX and INHERITANCE TAX etc.

Inland Revenue Pension Schemes Office (PSO) [UK]   See Pension Schemes Office of the Inland Revenue.

input tax [UK]   When a company or trader, registered for VALUE ADDED TAX (VAT), purchases goods or services from another supplier, VAT is additionally payable and is currently 17.5% of the purchase cost. This is known as input tax. Similarly, sales from the company or trader attract VAT at the same rate. This is known AS OUTPUT TAX. The difference between output tax and input tax is payable to the government department, Customs and Excise. In the event of input tax being greater than output tax, such as when starting up a new business, this difference is reclaimable from Customs and Excise.

insider dealing   The use of confidential company information (not known by any persons outside that company) by directors or staff in order to profit in share dealings. Such actions constitute a criminal offence.

insolvency   The inability of a person or company to settle debts when they become payable.

Institute of Financial Planning (IFP) [UK]   The UK professional body committed to the development of FINANCIAL PLANNING. The Institute was set up in 1986 and draws its members from accountancy, insurance, taxation, stockbroking, education and legal professions. Its stated objectives include 'promotion of the profession and practice of financial planning, increasing public awareness for the need for financial planning, creating of recognised professional qualifications for members, ensuring professional standards through a Code of Ethics and screening of new members, encouragement of education in the theory and practice of financial planning and the sharing of knowledge with other professionals'. A financial planner may be from any relevant professional background. To obtain Associate status a planner must hold a relevant professional qualification such as the Advanced Financial Planning Certificate (AFPC) and have three years related experience. Fellowship is available subject to the passing of a further examination and a longer period of experience. A list of Certified Financial Practitioners is established in the 'Registry' and is available to members of the public from the Institute. These practitioners are independent and are obliged to offer a fee basis. They must be prepared to offer a financial planning service separate from investment business if requested by a client. Reference to a Certified Financial Planner would usually be relevant to persons seeking a higher level of advice or those with more complex requirements.

institution   An organisation which invests the monies of its own investors. Such organisations are typically banks, insurance companies, mutual funds, unit trusts and pension funds etc and are very influential in the investment market due to the large sums of money at their disposal.

insurable interest   A term which means that any person entering into an insurance contract must stand to lose financially following the loss or damage of an insured item, or an insured event. For example a person may insure his/her property and contents since a financial loss would be incurred if damage were to be sustained.

insurance   A contract in which payment of premiums covers the INSURED against something which may, or may not occur. For example MOTOR INSURANCE covers the insured against accidents which may occur. In the UK insurance is differentiated from assurance (life assurance) which is protection against something which will inevitably occur.

insurance broker   A person specialising in insurance matters and who gives advice on the subject as well as arranging cover. Remuneration would normally be by way of commission from the INSURER.

Insurance Ombudsman   See Ombudsman.

insurance policy   The document which specifies the details and conditions of cover of an insurance contract together with the premium payable.

insurance premium   The amount payable by the INSURED in return for indemnification against specified risks.

insurance premium tax   A tax imposed on certain insurance premiums where the risk is located in the UK.

insured   A person or company acquiring insurance.

insurer   An authorised company which provides insurance.

intangible assets   Assets which are non physical in form, that is, which cannot be seen. Examples are patents, goodwill, trademarks and copyrights. See also tangible assets.

inter bank clearing The process of payment clearance between two banks.

inter branch clearing   The process of payment clearance between two branches of the same bank.

interest   The charge made for borrowed money. For example if a bank (the lender) lends money to a customer (the borrower) a charge will be made which is dependent on the INTEREST RATE in existence at the time of the loan. If a loan is made of say $1,000 at a rate of 10% per year, the interest payable is $100 per year. This does not take into consideration the repayment of the $1,000. The rate of interest may be variable or fixed. See simple interest. See compound interest.

interest in possession   The legal right to receive income from or occupy trust property.

interest only mortgage   A MORTGAGE where regular payments (usually monthly) only meet the interest requirements. The interest rate is usually variable and linked to prevailing rates but *can* be fixed for a given period. The capital amount outstanding remains approximately the same and the borrower will need to make additional provision for repaying this amount at the end of the term of the loan.

interest rate   The percentage rate at which INTEREST is charged on a loan for a period of one year.

interim   A term which means in the meantime. See interim bonus and interim dividend.

interim bonus [UK]   A bonus declared by life companies when maturity of a WITH PROFITS policy or death of the ASSURED occurs between normal BONUS DECLARATION dates.

interim dividend   The DIVIDEND declared before annual earnings are established. In the USA, a dividend is usually paid quarterly. Companies in the UK usually pay two dividends per year, the interim dividend and the FINAL DIVIDEND. The interim dividend is usually the smaller of the two.

intermediary   An AGENT, BROKER or financial institution who can give advice and act as a middle person between a company and a client conducting investment business.

Internal Revenue Service (IRS) [USA]   The US agency responsible for the collection of federal taxes which include personal and corporate income taxes, excise and gift taxes.

International Monetary Fund   A fund formed in the mid 1940s by industrialised countries to stabilise exchange rates, promote international trading and provide short term loans to member countries with BALANCE OF PAYMENTS problems.

international fund [USA]   A MUTUAL FUND whose portfolio comprises a range of securities from markets around the world.

International Petroleum Exchange (IPE) Europe's leading energy FUTURES and OPTIONS exchange and the second largest in the world. It provides a highly regulated market place where industry participants can manage their exposure to highly volatile energy prices. Incorporated in 1980, the IPE lists three main energy contracts: Brent Crude futures and options, Gas Oil futures and options and Natural Gas futures. The IPE is a Member owned exchange and clients can access the market either by becoming a Member or by using the broking services available from Members. Trades are cleared by the LONDON CLEARING HOUSE (LCH) which guarantees contract performance. The IPE is a RECOGNISED INVESTMENT EXCHANGE (RIE) regulated by the FINANCIAL SERVICES AUTHORITY (FSA)

International Stock Exchange of UK and Ireland See London Stock Exchange.

intestate The situation which exists when a person dies without making a will. The person is then said to have died intestate.

intrinsic value 1. An OPTIONS expression which indicates the difference between the current price of the UNDERLYING INSTRUMENT (for example a commodity or equity product) and the EXERCISE PRICE. A CALL OPTION has intrinsic value if the exercise price is below that of the underlying instrument and is said to be IN THE MONEY. If the exercise price of a PUT OPTION is below that of the underlying instrument there is no intrinsic value and it is said to be OUT OF THE MONEY. **2.** The difference between the current ordinary share price of a SECURITY and the EXERCISE PRICE of a WARRANT. If the exercise price is below the ordinary share price there is intrinsic value. If the exercise price is above the ordinary share price there is no intrinsic value. There may however be some TIME VALUE.

invalidity benefit [UK] A former state benefit payable after the expiry of state SICKNESS BENEFIT if a person was still unfit to work. This benefit was replaced by INCAPACITY BENEFIT in April 1995.

inventory 1. A company's finished goods, work in progress and raw materials. In the UK, an alternative to STOCK IN TRADE. **2.** An itemised list of an individual's assets.

investments The buying for example of shares or stock, shares in MUTUAL FUNDS, units in UNIT TRUSTS etc in order to make financial gain. The placing of money with banks and other financial institutions in order to earn INTEREST tends to be known as DEPOSIT TAKING BUSINESS. In the UK, the FINANCIAL SERVICES ACT 1986 defines investments to include shares, debentures and other securities such as government securities, certain options and warrants, unit trusts and other forms of collective investment schemes, futures contracts and some long term life insurance contracts. See investment business.

investment bond [UK] A unit linked single premium whole life assurance policy. Part of the premium gives life cover whilst the balance is invested in unitised funds. Under certain circumstances, since the bond is a life policy, certain tax advantages may be enjoyed. For example if the capital and annual interest are reinvested in full, there is no immediate liability to higher rate tax. If the proceeds of the bond are subsequently taken when a former higher rate taxpayer has become a basic rate payer, there is no higher rate tax liability. See unit linked policy.

investment business [UK] THE FINANCIAL SERVICES ACT 1986 defines investment business to include dealing, arranging deals in, managing and advising on investments in addition to the setting up and operation of collective investment schemes. See investments. See deposit taking business.

investment club A group of individuals who combine their capital and subsequently decide where investments are made, this usually being on a monthly or quarterly basis. The advantage of these clubs is that members' funds are invested in a range of securities thus reducing risk and fees. There are also the educational advantages. In the US, advice for starting up such clubs is available from the NATIONAL ASSOCIATION OF INVESTORS CORPORATION in Michigan. For the UK see ProShare.

investment company [USA] A company which invests the funds of small private investors in a range of securities. This enables fund shareholders to partake in ownership of a diversified portfolio of shares. Investment companies are classified as either OPEN END (MUTUAL FUND) or CLOSED END (INVESTMENT TRUST).

investment grade [USA] The description of a highly regarded bond with a rating of AAA to BBB.

investment income Income, paid from an investment, such as dividends and interest.

Investment Management Regulatory Organisation (IMRO) [UK] A SELF REGULATING ORGANISATION (SRO) with responsibility for monitoring the manner in which UK investment firms manage their funds, that is their client's investments. It supervises the way firms treat their clients and provide investment services. Companies include those which manage funds, unit trusts, ISAs and pension funds. IMRO is currently one of the three SROs (the other two being the PERSONAL INVESTMENT AUTHORITY [PIA] and the SECURITIES AND FUTURES AUTHORITY [SFA]) which report to the FINANCIAL SERVICES AUTHORITY (FSA). In due course the regulatory functions of the three SROs will be acquired by the FSA.

Investment Ombudsman See Ombudsman.

investment trust A company which invests its shareholders' funds in the shares of other companies. This enables small private investors to participate in ownership of a diversified portfolio of shares. Investment trusts are CLOSED END FUNDS, that is, there are a fixed number of shares in circulation, normally traded on a stock exchange, where prices are governed by what the market is prepared to pay, that is, by supply and demand. The value of a trust's assets less its liabilities is known as the NET ASSET VALUE (NAV). When the share price of a trust is less than the NAV it is said to trade at a DISCOUNT. This may be because the shares are not particularly in demand. If however the share price is higher than the NAV, the trust is said to trade at a PREMIUM. There is a wide variety of investment trusts available in which to invest with differing objectives.

Investor Protection Scheme See Building Societies Investor Protection Scheme.

Investors Compensation Scheme (ICS) [UK] A compensation scheme for investors with operating rules set by the FINANCIAL SERVICES AUTHORITY (FSA). The ICS may be able to assist private investors if the firm with whom an investment was made is fully authorised (see note) and has gone into default and cannot pay out claims. No compensation can be sought when investment values decrease as a result of market trends or inflation. The maximum amount claimable under the ICS is £48,000 which comprises the first £30,000 in full and 90% of the next £20,000. Note: An authorised firm must have satisfied its SRO, for example the PIA, that it is 'fit and proper' to conduct investment business. A list of authorised firms, known as the CENTRAL REGISTER is maintained by the FSA. However members of RECOGNISED PROFESSIONAL BODIES [RPBs] such as solicitors are not included in the ICS and operate their own compensation arrangements.

invoice A document, issued by a person or company, indicating to the recipient the amount of money owed to that person or company for goods and/or services supplied. When a number of transactions occur during a month between companies regularly, it is usual for a summary of invoices submitted to be tendered on a STATEMENT at the end of the month for overall settlement.

irredeemable securities [UK]   Securities, such as some DEBENTURES (perpetual debentures) and certain government loan stock (Consols) which do not have a redemption date that is there is no date specified for repayment of capital.

issue   1.   The number of shares of a company on sale to the public at a given time. **2.** A child mentioned in a will.

issue price   The price at which a company's shares are offered to the market for the first time. When they begin to be traded, the MARKET PRICE may be above or below the issue price. See new issue.

issued share capital   The amount of AUTHORISED SHARE CAPITAL that shareholders have actually subscribed to a company for share ownership.

issuing house   A financial INSTITUTION such as a MERCHANT BANK which provides its services to launch the shares of new companies on a stock exchange. It also ensures that the LISTING of such ISSUES complies with exchange regulations.

J

jobber [UK]   A dealer in shares prior to the event known as BIG BANG in October 1986. Jobbers dealt with investors only via stockbrokers who advised their clients on share transactions. After Big Bang, jobbers were replaced by MARKET MAKERS.

joint account   Typically a bank or brokerage account in the names of two (or more) persons. Arrangements can be made such that either individual or all signatures are required when drawing checks/cheques.

joint and several liability   An undertaking by a group of two or more persons to be responsible for any liability which may exist after any member or members have failed to meet their obligations. For example if a group of four persons enter into a joint and several liability on a bank loan, then in the event of two of the members reneging on their obligations the remaining two members become fully responsible for the repayment of the loan.

joint liability   The legal liability of two or more persons for claims against or debts incurred by them jointly. If three persons have joint liability and are indebted to another party, they may only be sued as a group and not individually.

joint life assurance [UK]   An assurance policy usually taken out on two lives, typically husband and wife. Under this type of policy, the SUM ASSURED is payable at the event of the first death.

joint ownership   Equal ownership of property by two or more persons. In the event of the death of one of the owners, title passes to the survivor (or survivors in equal amounts).

joint life annuity   Income usually relevant to two persons (for example man and wife) which continues until the death of the first person only.

joint life and survivor annuity   Income usually relevant to two persons (for example man and wife) which continues until the death of the second person.

joint tax return [USA]   A tax return completed and signed by two persons, usually a husband and wife. They have equal responsibility for taxes due. Filing a joint tax return can result in lower taxes than filing individually.

joint tenants   Two or more persons owning property. In the event of the death of one of the tenants, the property passes to the survivor(s).

judgement   A ruling by a court of law. An example is the ordering of a court to a person to settle a debt to another.

jumbo certificate of deposit [USA]   A certificate of deposit with a denomination of $100,000 and above. They are usually purchased by large institutions such as banks and insurance companies.

junk bonds   Bonds which offer high rates of interest but with correspondingly higher risk attached to the capital. In the US they carry a credit rating of BB and below.

K

kangaroos   A term for Australian shares with emphasis on mining, tobacco and land companies.

Keogh pension plan [USA]   A TAX DEFERRED retirement savings plan for the self employed.   Contributions are based on a percentage of earned income and are tax deductible.   Investment growth is tax deferred until the withdrawal of capital.

keyman / keywoman insurance   An insurance policy taken out on the life of a company executive or senior employee whose death would cause significant loss to the company.   In the event of such a death the proceeds of the policy would be payable to the company.

kiddie tax [USA]   A tax imposed on the investment income of children under the age of 14 where such income exceeds a certain level.   The tax level is the parents' highest rate.

knock for knock agreement   Although it currently rarely applies, this is a motor insurance term describing an agreement   between insurance companies where each pays the claims of its own clients following an accident.   This principle applies irrespective of blame and seeks to save time and expense.   One of the parties involved in such circumstances may however seek to sue the other and if successful may claim from the other's insurers.

know your customer [USA] know your client [UK]   The ethical principle relating to broker dealers and FINANCIAL ADVISERS that all reasonable steps have been taken to gather sufficient relevant financial and personal information regarding the customer and that subsequent investment recommendations will take full account of that information.

Krugerrand   A coin minted in South Africa containing one ounce of pure gold and originally intended as an investment item.

L

landlord   A property owner who rents it to another party called a tenant.

lapse   In insurance terminology, a policy is deemed to have lapsed when the policyholder fails to pay the renewal premiums. Also, it may be that the insurers do not invite renewal.

lapsed option [USA]   The expiry of an OPTION without being exercised by the holder. In the UK this is known as abandonment.

last trading day   An expression used in FUTURES and OPTIONS trading which refers to the last day for trading in a CONTRACT for a particular delivery or expiry month.

late charge [USA]   A charge imposed by a lender to a borrower when the borrower fails to make payment on the due date.

laundering   The manipulation of money obtained in a wrongful manner, for example theft, so as to seem to have originated from a lawful source. An example is to pay the unlawful money into an overseas bank and subsequently transfer back to the country of origin.

Law Society [UK]   The professional body for solicitors in England and Wales. Its aims and objectives are defined in the 1845 Royal Charter as having a responsibility to promote a 'professional improvement and facilitate the acquisition of legal knowledge'. The primary responsibility is to train and support solicitors to ensure they 'offer access to justice for all'. Also to enhance the reputation of the legal system by developing and maintaining standards in training and continuing education, admission of solicitors, professional ethics and investigation of complaints.

lease   A contract in which the legal owner of property or other asset agrees to another person using that property or asset in return for a regular specified payment (known as RENT) over a set term. In addition to buildings, other items such as cars and computers are often leased in order to avoid capital costs in the running of a business.

lease back   A situation whereby a property is sold by its owner to another person or company on condition that the purchaser leases the property back to the original owner for an agreed RENT over a set term. This enables the original owner to raise capital which can be used for other purposes.

leasehold land   Land which is rented from the owner for a specified term under a LEASE. At the expiry of the term the land reverts back to the owner.

ledger   A book in which the accounts of a business are kept. In the UK the main ledgers operating within a business are the *nominal ledger*, the *sales ledger* and the *purchase ledger*. The *nominal ledger* contains the nominal accounts which list revenue and operating expenses (for example building costs, vehicles etc) and the real accounts which detail the company's assets and capital. The *sales ledger* contains the sales accounts of customers and the *purchase ledger* contains the purchase accounts of suppliers. The sales accounts and purchase accounts are also known as personal accounts. In most businesses in current times such accounting information is stored in computers.

legacy   Another term for bequest, that is, the making of a gift by WILL. In the main there are three main types of legacy. *Pecuniary legacy:* A gift of a fixed sum of money left for example to an individual or a charity. *Specific legacy:* A gift of a specific item (such as a set of books) left for example to a friend. *Residuary legacy:* A gift consisting of the residue of an estate after all other conditions of the will have been met, or part of such residue.

legal expenses insurance   Insurance, taken out by individuals or companies for protection against defending civil actions brought about by other individuals or companies or alternatively to pursue them, where legal expenses (for example lawyer's fees) will be incurred.

legal list [USA]   A list of approved securities in which institutions such as savings banks, life insurance companies and pension funds may invest.

lender   A person or company that offers to lend money to a borrower for a given period of time. The borrower is obliged to repay the loan either by instalments or single payment together with specified interest.

lender of last resort   A prime function of a country's central bank. In the USA the lender of last resort is the FEDERAL RESERVE BANK. In the UK the BANK OF ENGLAND provides this role.

lessee   A person to whom a LEASE is granted, known as a TENANT.

lessor A person who grants a LEASE, known as a landlord.

letter of intent [USA] An undertaking by a shareholder in a MUTUAL FUND to make monthly investment payments for a period of one year. In return, the shareholder qualifies for a reduction in sales fees.

letter of renunciation In a RIGHTS ISSUE of shares, a letter of renunciation is the form attached to an ALLOTMENT LETTER which the holder completes should he/she wish to transfer entitlement to another person or to renounce his/her rights absolutely.

letter of wishes See memorandum of wishes.

letters of administration An order made by the court empowering the ADMINISTRATOR to settle the affairs of a deceased person in accordance with his/her WILL where an EXECUTOR has not been named or has predeceased (or fails to act for some other reason) and similarly when a person has died INTESTATE that is, a deceased person who has failed to make a will.

level annuity See annuity.

level term insurance See term life insurance (UK term assurance).

leverage In the US, the ratio of a company's LONG TERM DEBT, typically bonds and preferred stock, to its equity in its capital structure. The greater the long term debt, the greater the leverage. In the UK the term for leverage is GEARING.

leveraged buyout (LBO) The takeover of a company, financed by capital raised by the purchaser by heavy borrowing on the assets of the target company and its own assets.

liabilities The debts of a person or company. See current liabilities, long term liabilities, contingent liabilities.

liability insurance Insurance against legal liability to pay compensation and court costs where the INSURED has been found negligent in respect of injuries sustained by another person or damage to his/her property.

lien The right of an individual to retain possession of the goods of another until the latter fulfils his/her obligations such as the payment of an outstanding debt.

life insurance [USA] life assurance[UK]   An insurance policy which, in return for the payment of regular premiums, pays a lump sum on the death of the INSURED (UK LIFE ASSURED). In the case of CASH VALUE INSURANCE, in addition to life cover, a savings element provides benefits which are payable before death. In the UK ENDOWMENT ASSURANCE provides life cover or a maturity value after a specified term, whichever is the sooner.

life of another [UK]   A life assurance policy taken out on the life of another person by the policyholder. For example a man may take out a life assurance policy (where he is the policyholder that is, the ASSURED) on the life of his wife (the LIFE ASSURED) in order to cover various expenditures (for example a nanny for children) should the death of his wife occur.

limit order   An order to buy (for example shares) up to a maximum price or sell down to a minimum price. For example an investor may place a limit order to buy shares at $12 where the current price was say $15 and falling. If the price levels at $13 and goes up again the order would not be placed. Similarly if the price fell to $12 or below, the investor's order would be placed and the maximum he/she would pay would be $12.

limit price   The maximum buying price or minimum selling price a client is prepared to respectively pay or accept for shares or commodities etc.

limited company [UK]   A company whose shareholders' maximum liability is limited to their share capital in the event of winding up.

limited liability   The principle that the liability of shareholders for debts of a corporation or limited company is limited to the nominal value of their shares.

limited partnership   A partnership comprising a general partner and limited partners. The general partner operates the partnership and is fully liable for the debts of the firm. Limited partners receive some of the profits and have no influence in management. However their liabilities are limited to their original investment.

liquid assets   A company's cash plus assets which can readily be converted into cash.

liquid market   A market in which large quantities of shares (or commodities etc) are being bought and sold thereby making trading straightforward. This situation will also reduce the SPREAD that is, the difference between the buying and selling price of shares.

liquidation   The sale of a company's assets to settle as far as possible the debts to its CREDITORS prior to its winding up. Any cash left over is distributed to its shareholders.

liquidator   An official appointed to supervise the LIQUIDATION of a company.

liquidity   The ease with which assets can be sold to realise cash.

liquidity ratio   The ratio of LIQUID ASSETS to CURRENT LIABILITIES.

listed company [UK]   A company that has satisfied the requirements for its shares to be listed on a RECOGNISED INVESTMENT EXCHANGE (RIE). In the case of the LONDON STOCK EXCHANGE, a company which has obtained permission for its shares to be admitted to the DAILY OFFICIAL LIST.

listed firm [USA]   A company whose stock is traded on a leading stock exchange such as the NEW YORK STOCK EXCHANGE or AMERICAN STOCK EXCHANGE.

listed securities   Securities such as shares, stocks, bonds etc which are quoted on a leading stock exchange such as the NEW YORK STOCK EXCHANGE (NYSE) and the AMERICAN STOCK EXCHANGE in the USA and the LONDON STOCK EXCHANGE in the UK.

listing requirements [USA]]listing particulars [UK]   Details which a company is obliged to publish about itself together with any securities it issues before it obtains a listing on a recognised stock exchange.

litigation   The process of a person or company taking legal action against another.

Lloyds   The oldest and largest insurance market. Members are Lloyds brokers and syndicates of Lloyds underwriters forming a corporation. Business is obtained via Lloyds brokers dealing with the public which is underwritten by syndicates of Lloyds underwriters so organised as to spread risk. Members of syndicates are known as Names and must deposit a substantial sum of money (with unlimited risk attached) before acceptance. The main business is in marine insurance although virtually all other insurance (with the exception of life assurance) is covered.

load fund [USA]   A MUTUAL FUND in which shares are sold by a broker to an investor for a sales commission in return for which fund details would be explained.

loading **1.** A term for administration charges imposed by INSTITUTIONS on mutual funds, unit trusts and pension plans. See front end load and back end load. **2.** An addition to the premium for an insurance policy where extra risk is involved.

loan An advance of money from a lender to a borrower over a period of time. The borrower is obliged to repay the loan either at intervals during or at the end of the loan period together with interest.

loan account An ACCOUNT, opened for a customer by a bank, following the granting of a loan. The amount of the loan is credited to the customer's CURRENT ACCOUNT and similarly debited to the loan account. An arrangement is subsequently made for the customer to repay the loan, usually over a stated period of time, with interest additionally being paid on the outstanding amount.

loan capital [UK] That part of a company's capital structure which is raised by loans. Such loans (typically DEBENTURES) are usually over a stated period of time and pay fixed interest to the person making the loan. At the end of the period the capital is repaid. This contrasts with SHARE CAPITAL where shareholders are entitled to a proportion of the company's profits usually by way of DIVIDENDS. See gearing.

loan interest Interest payable on a loan. See interest.

loan protection policy An insurance policy in which the insured pays regular premiums in return for insurance against being unable to repay a loan due to accident, sickness or unemployment. In such an event the policy pays a benefit to assist the insured in making the repayments.

loan stock [UK] A security bearing a fixed rate of interest. The capital (the amount loaned) is repaid after a given period of time.

local authority investment A bond issued by a local authority in order to raise capital for its budget.

local taxes In the USA, taxes paid by an individual to a local state or county. These are deductible on the person's federal tax return. In the UK the nearest equivalent is the tax paid by houseowners to their local council (COUNCIL TAX). There is no tax relief on such payments but reductions can be claimed from the local council in cases where houseowners receive low income.

London Bullion

London Bullion Market   A two way market place in which investors can sell or buy both gold and silver. MARKET MAKERS mainly quote prices in US dollars per troy ounce for SPOT and forward delivery. FORWARD PRICES and OPTIONS quoted by market makers enable producers and industrial consumers to HEDGE their future commitments and provide access for investors and speculators.

London Bullion Market Association (LBMA)   An Association which represents the interests of the participants of the LONDON BULLION MARKET. One of its primary tasks is to ensure that Refiners of gold and silver meet the required standards of quality before their inclusion in the Market's Good Delivery lists. The Association maintains close links with the BANK OF ENGLAND, the latter being responsible for the supervision of the most active members of the market and for publishing the Code of Conduct by which all members are required to abide.

London Clearing House (LCH)   The LCH was founded in 1888 to clear sugar and coffee trades in London and was originally known as the London Produce Clearing House. It was renamed the International Commodities Clearing House (ICCH) in 1973 and went on to play a major role in serving and promoting futures and options markets in London and abroad. In 1991 it was renamed LCH at which time it separated from the group's non clearing businesses and concentrated on its primary role of acting as central counterparty for trades conducted on the futures and options markets in London. Once LCH has registered a trade, it becomes the buyer to every LCH Member who sells and seller to every LCH Member who buys, thereby guaranteeing that the financial obligations of trades are met. The LCH clears trades conducted on the INTERNATIONAL PETROLEUM EXCHANGE (IPE), the LONDON INTERNATIONAL FINANCIAL FUTURES EXCHANGE (LIFFE) incorporating the LONDON COMMODITY EXCHANGE (LCE), the TRADEPOINT INVESTMENT EXCHANGE and the LONDON METAL EXCHANGE (LME). The LCH is owned by the major UK clearing banks (Barclays, Lloyds, Midland, Natwest, Royal Bank of Scotland and Standard Chartered) and is a RECOGNISED CLEARING HOUSE under the regulatory supervision of the FINANCIAL SERVICES AUTHORITY (FSA).

London Commodity Exchange (LCE)   Formerly known as London Fox (London Futures and Options Exchange), the exchange was renamed London Commodity Exchange and was a FUTURES and OPTIONS exchange, dealing in soft commodities including cocoa, sugar, coffee, wheat, barley, potatoes and dry cargo freight futures that is, BIFFEX (Baltic International Freight Futures Exchange). BIFFEX was merged with the then London Fox in 1991. On 16th September 1996 the LCE merged with the London International Financial Futures and Options Exchange (LIFFE) where trades of the merged company are guaranteed by the LONDON CLEARING HOUSE (LCH). See London International Financial Futures and Options Exchange (LIFFE).

London Inter Bank Offered Rate (LIBOR)   The rate of interest at which banks will lend money to each other.

London International Financial Futures and Options Exchange (LIFFE)   A FUTURES and OPTIONS exchange, located in London, which originally dealt solely in financial instruments including equities (shares), government bonds, indices (such as the FT-SE 100 Index) interest rates and a wide range of currencies. On 16th September 1996, LIFFE merged with the then LONDON COMMODITY EXCHANGE with unified administration and exchange systems. LIFFE Commodity products for futures and options trading are No. 7 Cocoa, Robusta Coffee, No. 5 White Sugar, Wheat, Barley, Potato and BIFFEX (Baltic freight). All trades of the merged exchange are guaranteed by the LONDON CLEARING HOUSE (LCH). LIFFE is a RECOGNISED INVESTMENT EXCHANGE (RIE), regulated by the FINANCIAL SERVICES AUTHORITY (FSA).

London Metal Exchange (LME)   An international market, located in London, for the trading of non-ferrous metals, namely copper, primary aluminium, aluminium alloy, lead, nickel, tin and zinc, primarily for industrial use. Its prime function is HEDGING with 70-80% of turnover originating from trade clients. Other dealings include FUTURES and OPTIONS contracts and ARBITRAGE trading. THE LONDON CLEARING HOUSE (LCH) acts as guarantor to trades conducted between CLEARING MEMBERS. The LME is a RECOGNISED INVESTMENT EXCHANGE (RIE), regulated by the FINANCIAL SERVICES AUTHORITY (FSA).

London Securities and Derivatives Exchange (OMLX)   An integrated exchange and CLEARING HOUSE for FUTURES and OPTIONS DERIVATIVES based mainly on the Swedish and Norwegian equity markets. Products include futures and options on the OMX Swedish equity index (the 30 most liquid shares traded on the Stockholm Stock Exchange), the OBX Norwegian equity index (the 25 most traded stocks on the Oslo Stock Exchange), Swedish equity futures and options and Norwegian equity futures and options. There is a further futures and options market based on wood pulp (known as Pulpex) currently being established at OMLX in London. OMLX is a wholly owned subsidiary of OM Gruppen AB of Stockholm. Another subsidiary, OM Stockholm, interlinks with OMLX, the Oslo Stock Exchange and the Norwegian Futures and Options Clearing House to provide real time trading and clearing.

OMLX is a Recognised Investment Exchange (RIE), regulated by the Financial Services Authority (FSA).

London Stock Exchange   The UK market-place for the trading of LISTED SECURITIES (shares, government stocks [gilts], bonds etc). It maintains market rules and regulations and provides a range of services for market users. Over 7000 securities are bought and sold, where the main markets are UK and international equities. Trading in the various securities is by way of MARKET MAKERS who are required to make buying and selling prices for the securities in which they are registered. In order for a company to be admitted to the Exchange it must make application for a place on the 'OFFICIAL LIST'. This involves providing extensive data regarding its financial status and trading history etc. The London Stock Exchange is a RECOGNISED INVESTMENT EXCHANGE under the regulatory supervision of the FINANCIAL SERVICES AUTHORITY (FSA).

long   See long position.

long bond [USA]   In the USA, a bond with a maturity of more than ten years. Also the US 30 year Treasury bond.

long position   The purchase of a security, commodity or financial instrument (for example, currencies etc) in the belief that the price will increase. The purchaser would then hope to sell it at a higher price and thus make a profit. See short position.

long term debt [USA]   Debt liabilities due in one year or more.

long term care insurance   The planning, by way of suitable insurance, for covering partially or in full, the cost of long term care in old age. The place of care may be the insured's own residence or a nursing home. In order to claim benefit, the INSURED must be disabled to the extent that he/she is unable to perform say three daily activities such as washing, dressing and eating/drinking.

long term gain [USA]   A gain on a capital asset relating to a holding period of more than one year.

long term liabilities   Debts of a company which are not due for repayment in the next accounting period.

longs [UK]   1. REDEEMABLE GILTS or bonds with a REDEMPTION DATE beyond fifteen years. **2.** Securities (for example, shares), commodities or financial instruments (for example, indices, currencies etc) held in a LONG POSITION.

loss of income insurance [USA]   Insurance in which the INSURED is covered against loss of income.

lot   An alternative expression for contract in FUTURES and OPTIONS trading. See contract 2.

low cost endowment assurance   See endowment assurance.

low cost whole life assurance   See whole of life assurance.

low start endowment assurance   See endowment assurance.

lower earnings limit [UK]   That level of income at which employees start to pay CLASS 1 NATIONAL INSURANCE CONTRIBUTIONS .

lower rate tax   The lowest rate of income tax in the UK, currently 20%.

lump sum   A sum of money paid in a single instalment.

luxury tax [USA]   A tax on goods considered to be luxury items.

M

M0, M1, M2, M3, M4, L.   See money supply.

macroeconomics   The study of a country's economy using such elements as unemployment, price levels, government spending, interest rates, national productivity etc and the influence of government policy on them.

maintenance payments [UK]   Money paid by a divorced or separated man to his ex wife to assist her with living expenses. (In unusual circumstances payment could be made by the wife to her ex husband). From the taxation point of view, maintenance may be enforceable following a court order, or voluntary. Where maintenance is enforceable the recipient will, under certain circumstances, be liable for tax, depending on when the order was made and the amount paid. The person making the payments can claim limited tax relief. For voluntary payments, the recipient is not liable for tax and the person making the payments cannot claim tax relief.

making a market   In the USA, the sustaining of firm bid and asked ROUND LOT quotes at which a dealer is obliged to buy and sell, for a specified security. An exchange dealer is known as a SPECIALIST and an over the counter dealer is called a MARKET MAKER. See making a price.

making a price   In the UK, a term used on the LONDON STOCK EXCHANGE which refers to the obligation of a MARKET MAKER to quote a broker both a price at which he/she is willing to purchase a SECURITY and a price at which he/she is willing to sell. The market maker would not normally be aware as to whether the enquirer wishes to buy or sell but once the prices have been given they must be honoured if the broker wishes to deal.

managed account   An investment account, managed by the investment department of a bank for a client.

managed fund   A UNIT LINKED fund managed by a LIFE ASSURANCE company. The fund is invested in a wide range of securities so as to keep risk to a minimum.

management charges   Charges made by the managers of, for example, a MUTUAL FUND or UNIT TRUST which include for investment management and administration costs etc.

mandate   An official order from an authority to implement an action.

mandatory quote period   A term used on the LONDON STOCK EXCHANGE which refers to the period of time during which MARKET MAKERS in a security are obliged to display their prices. For SEAQ (STOCK EXCHANGE AUTOMATED QUOTATIONS system), the period is from 8.30am to 4.30pm.

margin   **1.** The difference between the cost price of a product and the selling price. See gross margin. **2.** In securities trading, the amount deposited with a broker in order to obtain credit for purchase of a security (securities). The margin is the price of a security less credit advanced by the broker. **3.** The difference between a MARKET MAKER'S buying and selling prices. Also known as SPREAD. **4.** In futures trading, the amount which must be deposited by an investor prior to trading.

margin account   An account with a broker where a client is able to purchase securities on credit after MARGIN has been deposited.

margin call   A demand from a broker to a client to provide more funds to bring a MARGIN ACCOUNT balance up to a required level.

margin securities   Securities which may be bought or sold on MARGIN. In the USA, an approved list of margin securities is published by the Federal Reserve Board.

marginal tax rate   The additional tax paid on each unit (for example dollar or pound) increase of taxable income.

market   **1.** A place for the buying and selling of goods and services. **2.** A gathering of traders within an exchange, where securities are bought and sold, for example the NEW YORK STOCK EXCHANGE or the LONDON STOCK EXCHANGE.

market capitalisation   The approximate value of a company which is calculated by multiplying its total issued shares by the current share price. This value will constantly change in accordance with any increase or decrease in the share price.

making a market   In the USA, the sustaining of firm bid and asked ROUND LOT quotes at which a dealer is obliged to buy and sell, for a specified security. An exchange dealer is known as a SPECIALIST and an over the counter dealer is called a MARKET MAKER.

market maker   A dealer in securities who is obliged to offer buying and selling prices for those securities in which he/she deals. These prices must be honoured if a broker decides to deal. In the USA, 'market maker' is the term often given to a dealer in the over the counter market. An exchange (for example the New York Stock Exchange) dealer is known as a SPECIALIST.   In the UK, the term 'market maker' is given to those dealing on a main exchange such as the London Stock Exchange.

market order   An order to buy or sell SECURITIES or COMMODITIES   at the best price with immediate effect.

market price   The price for a security. There is however a market price for selling and a market price for buying and when quoted in newspapers etc the value is usually an average of these. In the UK, this is also known as the MID PRICE. The difference between the buying and selling prices is known as the SPREAD or MARGIN.

marital deduction [USA]   The provision for tax free transference of property between spouses irrespective of value. In the UK this is similarly the case

Mastercard   An international payment services and card scheme.

maturity   The capital repayment date of a BOND. Also the end of the term of a CASH VALUE INSURANCE policy (endowment assurance policy in the UK).

means test   An appraisal of a person's income and assets to establish if he/she qualifies for state benefits.

medical insurance   See health insurance (USA). See private medical insurance (UK).

mediums [UK]   REDEEMABLE GILTS or bonds with a REDEMPTION DATE (maturity date) between five and fifteen years.

medium term bond [USA]   A bond with a maturity between two and ten years. In the UK medium term bonds are popularly known as MEDIUMS.

member bank [USA]   A bank which is a member of the FEDERAL RESERVE SYSTEM.

member firm [USA] A brokerage firm that has a minimum of one member on a stock exchange whereby the membership is in the name of an individual and not the firm. **[UK]** A trading firm of brokers or market makers which is a member of the London Stock Exchange. Member firms may deal in shares on behalf of itself or on behalf of its clients.

memorandum of association [UK] Those details which a company, when formed, must submit to the Registrar of Companies together with its articles of association. They include company name, registered office, object, authorised share capital and a statement of limited liability etc.

memorandum of wishes (letter of wishes) A memorandum or letter addressed to the executors of a will by the testator (feminine testatrix), that is, the maker of the will, specifying additional wishes to be carried out. For example a woman may leave her jewellery to her executor with a letter of wishes requesting that they pass certain items to named individuals.

merchant A trader who purchases goods for resale in home or foreign markets.

merchant bank A bank which offers a range of services including the raising of capital for companies, advice on international trading, takeovers and mergers and flotations etc.

microeconomics The study of economic elements at the level of the household or the company. Persons within a household are primarily concerned with employment prospects and how taxation affects their income. Companies are mainly concerned with product costs and operating expenses etc. See macroeconomics.

middle price See mid price.

mid price The average of the bid price and offer price of a security.

minimum contributions See appropriate personal pension plan.

minimum maintenance [USA] The minimum amount of equity which must be kept in a margin account as specified by the New York Stock Exchange, the National Association of Securities Dealers and brokerage firms.

minimum quote size   A LONDON STOCK EXCHANGE term which refers to the minimum number of shares in which market makers must display prices on the SEAQ for those securities for which they are registered.

monetary policy   The control of the MONEY SUPPLY and interest rates by a government in order to achieve its economic objectives, in particular the restraining of INFLATION. See fiscal policy.

money   A medium of exchange usually consisting of coins and bank notes.

money broker   A type of AGENT who arranges short term loans between banks (which are seeking to lend money) and borrowers such as institutions. The money broker is not involved in the process of lending/borrowing but merely acts as an intermediary earning a commission.

money laundering   See laundering.

money market   A market in which money and other LIQUID ASSETS such as BILLS OF EXCHANGE and TREASURY BILLS can be lent and borrowed in order to satisfy the short term (from overnight to several months) CASH FLOW requirements of banks and other institutions. Where personal investors have large sums of money to deposit, they can also gain access to the money market via the commercial banks.

money purchase scheme (defined contributions scheme)   A PENSION scheme in which the benefits will be dependent on contributions to and growth of the fund and the fund manager's costs. See occupational pension. See personal pension.

money supply   The total amount of money in an economy at a given time.

[USA]   The main measures of money supply are M1, M2, M3 and L.

M1:   The amount of notes and coins in circulation plus DEMAND DEPOSITS   (checking accounts from which money can be withdrawn on demand). Also referred to as narrow money.

M2:   Includes all M1 items plus savings deposits of $100,000 or below.

M3:   Includes all M2 items plus savings deposits over $100,000.

L: Includes all M3 items plus government securities such as treasury notes and savings bonds.

[UK]   The main measures of money supply are M0 and M4.

M0:   Sterling notes and coins in circulation outside the Bank of England including those held in tills of banks and building societies plus banks' operational deposits with the Bank of England. Also known as narrow money.

M4:   M0 plus all sterling deposits at UK monetary financial institutions held in the M4 private sector. Also known as broad money.

money transmission   The process of transferring funds and making payments.

mortgage   A loan whereby the borrower (the mortgagor) offers a property and land as SECURITY (2.) to the lender (the mortgagee) until the loan is repaid. Repayments of the loan are usually made on a monthly basis over a long period of time, typically 25 years. In the UK, the most common forms of mortgage are the REPAYMENT MORTGAGE and the INTEREST ONLY MORTGAGE.

mortgage backed security [USA]   A security, backed by a pool of mortgages, whereby the shareholder receives payments based on the interest and principal paid on the underlying mortgages.

mortgage broker [USA]   A person or company engaged in the arrangement of mortgages for buyers. The broker is usually paid a commission by the lender.

mortgage indemnity guarantee protection   An additional one off payment, made by the borrower of a mortgage (the mortgagor), which, via an insurance policy, protects the lender (such as a bank) when repossessing a property where the sale price is less than the mortgage outstanding. Any such shortfall will be claimed by the lender off the policy.

mortgage interest deduction [USA]   An allowable federal tax deduction for the annual interest paid on a mortgage.

mortgage interest relief at source (MIRAS) [UK]   Interest paid on the first £30,000 of a MORTGAGE qualifies for INCOME TAX relief. This is usually claimed through mortgage interest relief at source which means that the lender (for example a bank or building society) deducts the amount of income tax relief and the borrower pays the net amount, normally monthly.

mortgage life insurance   A LIFE INSURANCE policy which pays off the outstanding balance of a mortgage in the event of the death of the INSURED.

mortgage protection [UK]   TERM ASSURANCE to cover the repayment of a mortgage in the event of the death of the mortgagor (the person who takes out the mortgage) during the period of the loan. In the case of a REPAYMENT MORTGAGE the capital sum outstanding is gradually reduced over the term of the loan (albeit slowly during the initial years when the majority of the repayments are paying the interest) so that DECREASING TERM ASSURANCE would be incorporated in the policy. For an ENDOWMENT MORTGAGE where the SUM ASSURED and the death benefit are at least equal to the amount of the loan throughout the term of the loan, LEVEL TERM ASSURANCE would be apt.

mortgagee   A company or institution such as a bank or building society (that is, the lender) which advances a loan which is secured by a property and the land on which it is built.

mortgagor   A person or company who takes out a loan and offers a property and the land on which it is built as security.

motor insurance [UK]   The insurance of motor vehicles covering damage or loss and liabilities for injuries to other persons and damage to property. It is a legal requirement that drivers are insured against THIRD PARTY claims that is, THIRD PARTY INSURANCE. Under this type of insurance, if it is proven that the insured is the cause of an accident, the insurance company will only pay for injury or repairs for damage to the property of the third party. A variant of this is third party fire and theft insurance which is basically third party insurance plus additional cover if the insured's vehicle is damaged by fire or if stolen. For a somewhat higher premium, comprehensive insurance gives additional cover to the INSURED including damage to his/her vehicle, personal effects and overseas travel etc. Known as automobile insurance in the USA.

Motor Insurers' Bureau (MIB) [UK]   An organisation formed in 1946 which provides a means of compensating victims of road accidents caused by uninsured or untraceable drivers. Persons who are the victims of accidents caused by uninsured motorists may claim for bodily injury and property damage. Persons who are the victims of accidents caused by untraced motorists may claim for bodily injury only. The effective cost to the motor policy holder is currently around 1.5% of the premium paid.

municipal bond [USA]   A bond issued by a state or local government often to pay for a special project such as a highway. In certain cases, interest is tax exempt.

municipal bond insurance [USA]   An insurance policy which guarantees a mutual bond in the case of default, issued by private insurers.

municipal note [USA]   A municipal debt obligation with a maturity of two years or less.

mutual company   See mutual organisation.

mutual fund [USA]   A collective investment scheme, operated by an INVESTMENT COMPANY, which enables small private investors to partake in ownership of a diversified portfolio of shares, bonds and other securities. It is known as an OPEN END fund since there is no fixed amount of CAPITAL in the fund. Funds are managed by professional fund managers who invest in securities to achieve the trust's objectives such as capital growth, income or a combination of both. Shares purchased from brokers are called LOAD FUNDS and those purchased direct from the fund company are called NO LOAD FUNDS. Shares when sold are redeemed at their NET ASSET VALUE. There is a wide range of funds with a variety of objectives available in which to invest including capital growth and income. Similar to a UNIT TRUST in the UK.

mutual fund custodian [USA]   A commercial bank or trust company that safeguards securities held by a mutual fund.

mutual organisation (mutual company)   An organisation which is owned by its policyholders, that is, there are no shareholders. Policyholders receive a share in the profits of the organisation.

mutual savings bank [USA]   A savings bank which is owned by its depositors.

N

naked   An expression describing the position of the WRITER of an OPTION which is not covered by an opposite position in the UNDERLYING INSTRUMENT (for example shares, commodities etc).

narrow market   A market in which the trading of shares is only light. Slight movement in activity can result in exaggerated price fluctuations.

narrow money   Another name for M1 in the USA and M0 in the UK (see money supply).

Nasdaq   The first electronic stock market created, using computers and telecommunications to trade shares rather than a traditional trading floor. Nasdaq is owned and operated by the National Association of Securities Dealers (NASD). It is the fastest growing major stock market in the world with well over 5,000 companies listed. MARKET MAKERS compete to buy and sell Nasdaq listed stocks of U.S. and non-U.S. based companies via a worldwide computer network for large and small investors.   Nasdaq International, a U.K. based subsidiary of Nasdaq, assists non U.S. companies to list on the Nasdaq Stock Market. It is based in London and additionally provides a variety of information including services for investors, public relations and background on Nasdaq.

National Association of Investors Corporation (NAIC) [USA]   A non profit association, located in Michegan, which provides advice to INVESTMENT CLUBS.

National Association of Securities Dealers (NASD)   See Nasdaq.

National Credit Union Administration [USA]   An independent federal agency which supervises federal credit unions and insures members deposits.

national debt   The debt of a government in respect of its borrowing from its own population and from overseas bodies.

National Girobank   See Girobank plc.

National Insurance [UK]   A form of taxation, payable by employees, employers and the self employed, which is notionally to fund state benefits including pensions, sickness, unemployment and maternity. It is part of the state's social security system and ultimately controlled by the Department of Social Security. See also Benefits Agency and Contributions Agency.

National Insurance (NI) Basic Pension [UK]   The basic state PENSION funded by a person's NATIONAL INSURANCE CONTRIBUTIONS over his/her working life and part of the NATIONAL INSURANCE PENSION. The rate at which the basic pension is paid is dependent on the person's NATIONAL INSURANCE CONTRIBUTIONS record also over his/her working life.

National Insurance (NI) Contributions [UK]   There are currently four categories of contributions: Class 1, Class 2, Class 3 and Class 4.

Class 1: Employees earning above the LOWER EARNINGS LIMIT pay contributions at a rate dependent on their income and whether they are contracted in or out of SERPS. The contributions are made up to the UPPER EARNINGS LIMIT, that is, no NI contributions are payable on earnings above this limit. In addition to employees' contributions, employers must pay Class 1 contributions on all the employees' earnings.

Class 2: Self employed persons pay flat rate Class 2 contributions provided profits are above a certain level.

Class 3: These are voluntary contributions which can make up for unpaid contributions over the previous six years.

Class 4: Self employed persons also pay a percentage of profits made between given limits.

National Insurance (NI) Pension (State Pension) [UK]   The state PENSION which is payable to persons at retirement age currently 60 for women and 65 for men. There are two main pensions; the NI BASIC PENSION and the STATE EARNINGS RELATED PENSION SCHEME (SERPS) which is also known as Additional Pension. There is also a benefit payable additionally to the NI Pension namely the Graduated Pension or Graduated Retirement Benefit. This was a state scheme which existed between April 1961 and April 1975 for persons earning over £9 per week. Persons who were employees during any part of this period and who paid Graduated NI Contributions will receive a Graduated Retirement Benefit. Women over 60 and men over 65 can if they wish continue in employment even when they are receiving the NI Pension. See pension forecast.

National Savings [UK]   A variety of savings schemes, backed by the government, in which the public can participate. National Savings publishes a booklet entitled *'Investor's Guide'* which describes in detail how it operates and the products it offers. Leaflets covering individual savings schemes and up to date interest rates are available from Post Office branches. The savings schemes currently include, *Capital Bonds, Income Bonds, FIRST Option Bonds, Pensioners Bonds, Children's Bonus Bonds, Investment Account, Ordinary Account, Fixed Interest Savings Certificates, Index Linked Savings Certificates and Premium Bonds.*

National Savings Bank [UK]   The savings bank operated by the government's Department of National Savings. The majority of business is carried out via the Post Office.

National Savings Bonds   See National Savings.

National Savings Certificates   See National Savings.

National Savings Stock Register [UK]   A register of government stocks (GILTS) which can be purchased by the public through the Post Office at favourable rates of commission for moderate purchases and sales. Transactions are conducted by mail and interest is paid gross and is taxable. Despite the name, the Register is now administered by the BANK OF ENGLAND.

negative equity [UK]   A situation where the purchaser of a property has taken out a MORTGAGE and some time after the purchase, the value of the property falls below the mortgage amount. For example, Purchase price of property: £80,000. Deposit: £10,000. Mortgage: £70,000 If the current sale price were to fall to below £70,000, say £68,000, a negative equity of £2,000 would exist, that is, in the event of a sale, the property seller would end up owing the provider of the mortgage £2,000. In addition there would be other legal and agents fees to be paid. The original deposit of £10,000 would also be lost.

negotiable   An instrument, such as a CHEQUE or a BILL OF EXCHANGE, where the PAYEE can transfer the value to another person by inserting that person's name or by signing on the reverse side.

negotiable instrument   A document, such as a check or bill of exchange by which funds are transferred from one person to another.

net   The return on investments such as savings accounts and fixed interest securities after deduction of tax.

net assets   The total ASSETS of a company (CURRENT ASSETS plus FIXED ASSETS) less its CURRENT LIABILITIES.

net asset value (NAV) [USA]   In mutual funds, the net value per share.
[UK]   The total ASSETS of a company less all its LIABILITIES including LOAN CAPITAL and PREFERENCE SHARES. Usually expressed in pence per share.

For example,
        assets of a company = £12,000,000, liabilities = £3,000,000,
                    number of ordinary shares = 18,000,000.
    NAV = (£12,000,000 - £3,000,000) / 18,000,000 = 50p per share.

The term is used particularly when valuing companies
such as INVESTMENT TRUSTS.

net income [USA]   Net profit. Also income received by a person after the deduction of tax. GROSS INCOME less TAX ALLOWANCES = TAXABLE INCOME. Net income = Gross income less tax.

net profit   The GROSS PROFIT of a company (total turnover of products sold less costs to purchase or manufacture) less all other expenses. Net profit is usually expressed before or after tax, that is, NET PROFIT BEFORE TAX or NET PROFIT AFTER TAX. Often the 'net' is dispensed with in company accounts.

net profit after tax (profit after tax)   The net profits of a company after taxation. If applicable, DIVIDENDS are normally paid at this stage.

net profit before tax (pre tax profit)   The net profits of a company immediately prior to taxation.

net relevant earnings [UK]   A person's non pensionable income (that is, income from employment where no pension scheme exists) plus taxable BENEFITS IN KIND less any allowable business expenses but before deduction of PERSONAL ALLOWANCES. For self employed persons these are taxable profits less CAPITAL ALLOWANCES or losses from previous years.

net yield   The YIELD on a security (such as shares, bonds etc) after the deduction of tax.

new issue   The offering of a company's shares to the market via a stock exchange for the first time or the issuing of additional shares.

New York Mercantile Exchange (NYM)   Following the merger with the Commodity Exchange (COMEX) in 1994, the exchange operates two divisions that is, NYMEX which deals in futures and options on a number of products including crude oil, heating oil and platinum and COMEX which deals in futures and options on copper, gold and silver.

New York Stock Exchange (NYSE)   The principal stock exchange of the US, located on Wall Street where over 2,000 common and preferred stocks are traded.

Nikkei Dow Index   An index of the average value of the shares of 225 Japanese companies which reflects share price movement on the Tokyo Stock Exchange. The index is weighted according to price so smaller companies can influence the index as much as the larger ones.

nil paid   A new issue of shares where no payment has yet been made. This normally applies following a RIGHTS ISSUE.

nil shares   A company's newly issued shares which can normally be transferred on a RENOUNCEABLE DOCUMENT.

no claim bonus   A bonus which is awarded to a policy holder when no claims have been made on an insurance policy during the period of insurance, usually one year. The bonus is subsequently applied to reduce the renewal premium. The motor insurance business uses this approach extensively and companies will usually increase no claim bonuses annually up to a maximum, typically 60%, after four or five years. This method of rewarding policy holders with no claims is sometimes used in HOUSEHOLD INSURANCE.

no load fund [USA]   A MUTUAL FUND where investors deal directly with the investment company rather than through a broker. Investors are accordingly not charged a sales commission and the net asset value, bid and offer prices are equal.

no par value (NPV)   The shares of a company which carry no NOMINAL PRICE or PAR VALUE.

nominal account   An account kept in a LEDGER which itemises revenue and expenditure such as sales and operating costs (building running costs, maintenance of vehicles etc).

nominal income [USA]   Income which does not take account of changes in the PURCHASING POWER of the dollar.

nominal ledger   A ledger which contains the NOMINAL ACCOUNTS and REAL ACCOUNTS of a company.

nominal price   The price of a security (stocks, shares, bonds etc) when issued which bears no relation to the MARKET PRICE. Also known as face value or par value.

nominal value   See nominal price.

nominal yield   See yield.

nominee   A person or company nominated by another to act on his/her behalf regarding the holding of securities. See street name. See beneficial owner.

nominee account   An account operated on behalf of a person (the BENEFICIAL OWNER) for the holding of securities.

nominee company   A company formed by a bank or other organisation which operates NOMINEE ACCOUNTS that is, the holding of shares for the BENEFICIAL OWNER.

non contributory pension plan   A pension plan in which an employee does not make contributions. The plan is funded totally by the employer.

non forfeiture clause   A clause in a life insurance policy which lays out the conditions under which the policy may remain in force for a limited period if the premium remains unpaid after the expiry of the DAYS OF GRACE.

non participating life insurance policy [USA]   Life insurance which does not pay dividends.

non qualifying life policy [UK]   A life assurance policy which does not satisfy the requirements of the Inland Revenue and does not qualify for certain tax relief. See qualifying policy.

normal market size (NMS) [UK]   The SEAQ method of classifying shares on the LONDON STOCK EXCHANGE. This method replaced the previous alpha, beta, gamma, delta shares system which was a reflection of the order of the most actively traded shares. NMS is a value expressed as a number of shares which is applied to determine the minimum quote size for each share.

normal retirement age [UK]   The age at which an individual normally retires (60 to 70 for men and 55 to 70 for women). Men qualify for the state pension at 65 and women currently qualify at 60. However the qualifying normal retirement age for women will be increasing depending on their date of birth, the scale applying for those born after 6th April 1950. For PERSONAL PENSION PLANS individuals may take retirement between the ages of 50 and 75 and for RETIREMENT ANNUITIES between the ages of 60 and 75.

normal trading unit USA]   The normal size of a securities order. A normal trading unit for shares is 100. Also called a round lot. Known as an odd lots where trades of shares are below 100.

not negotiable   Words written on a BILL OF EXCHANGE or CHEQUE which prevents enactment following theft. For example if A writes a cheque to B and marks it 'not negotiable', then in the event that the cheque is stolen by C, it could not be cashed since no one can have a good title to it other than B.

note [USA]   A DEBT INSTRUMENT whereby the issuer promises repayment on or before a specified date.

notice of assignment   See allocation notice.

NYMEX   The division of the NEW YORK MERCANTILE EXCHANGE which deals in crude oil, heating oil and platinum FUTURES and OPTIONS.

occupational pension plan   A pension plan operated by a company or organisation for the benefit of its employees. The employer and employee contribute to a fund which grows free of tax during the savings period. There are two main types of pension fund, that is, DEFINED CONTRIBUTIONS PLAN or DEFINED BENEFIT PLAN. At retirement the employee draws an income which is subject to tax.

Occupational Pensions Regulatory Authority (OPRA) [UK]   The Authority set up under the Pensions Act 1995 to make OCCUPATIONAL PENSIONS more secure. OPRA commenced operations on 6th April 1997. It regulates pension schemes by ensuring that those persons who operate them conform to a wide range of rules. These include how trustees may be chosen, information to scheme members, a complaints system and keeping of records etc. OPRA investigates situations where dishonesty or carelessness may be detrimental to retirement plans of persons within such occupational schemes and where rules are broken.

odd lot [USA]   The trading of securities at lots less than 100, that is, less than the normal unit.

offer   The price indicated by a seller at which he/she is prepared to sell an item.

offer for sale   A company's invitation to the public to purchase its shares.

offer price [USA]   **1.** The price per share of a MUTUAL FUND. This is the NET ASSET VALUE in a NO LOAD FUND. If a LOAD FUND, the share price is the net asset value plus a sales charge.   **2.** The price at which a new issue of shares is offered to the public.   **[UK]** The price at which a MARKET MAKER will sell a security (stocks, shares, bonds etc) or the price at which units can be purchased from an INSTITUTION in a UNIT TRUST. See bid price.

offer to bid   A term often used in the UK which enables an investor to establish the growth of his/her investment. It is a comparison between a previous OFFER PRICE (the price the investor paid) of a UNIT TRUST and the current BID PRICE (the price the investor would receive if units were sold). This comparison allows an investor to see exactly how well his/her investment has performed over the period of time in question (for example, over one, three or five years etc).

Office of Thrift Supervision (OTS) [USA]   An agency of the US Treasury Department with responsibility for overseeing the savings and loans industry.

Official List   See Daily Official List.

offshore   The location of a financial institution's subsidiary outside its lawful DOMICILE.

offshore funds   Assets invested offshore (for example the Bahamas or the Channel Islands) where tax advantages exist. However gains are subject to the taxation rules of an investor's domicile (permanent country of residence).

Old Lady of Threadneedle Street   A traditional name for the BANK OF ENGLAND, located in Threadneedle Street, London.

Ombudsman [UK]   An independent official appointed to investigate the complaints of individuals against companies within the financial services industry. In the first instance complaints need to be registered (preferably in writing) with the COMPLIANCE officer or senior management of the company in question. If the outcome is unsatisfactory to the individual, reference can then be made to the applicable Ombudsman. These include the *Banking Ombudsman*, the *Building Societies Ombudsman*, the *Insurance Ombudsman*, the *Investment Ombudsman*, the *Pensions Ombudsman* the *PIA Ombudsman*. **2.** An official appointed to investigate complaints of individuals against public authorities.

OPAS [UK]   An abbreviation for Occupational Pensions Advisory Service. However since personal pension plans are now included, the organisation is additionally known as the Pensions Advisory Service. OPAS is a voluntary independent organisation which receives grants from the DSS. It is staffed by a number of professional volunteer pension advisers who will help members of the public who have a complaint regarding their OCCUPATIONAL PENSION SCHEME or PERSONAL PENSION PLAN.

open end fund   Typically a MUTUAL FUND or UNIT TRUST or OPEN ENDED INVESTMENT COMPANY (OEIC). There is no fixed amount of capital in the fund, that is, there is no limit on the number of shares or units the fund or trust can issue and the volume varies up or down according to the buying and selling activities of the investors.

open ended investment company (OEIC) [UK]   A collective investment scheme enabling investors to partake in ownership of a diversified portfolio of shares. An OEIC is a version of a UNIT TRUST and is a structured company with investors holding shares rather than units as in a unit trust. The company is open ended in that it can expand or contract according to demand and thus has a variable size. The price paid for shares reflects the value of the underlying assets and there is a single price for buying and selling. Commissions and management charges are disclosed separately. (A unit trust has a buying [offer] price and a selling [bid] price, the difference taking account of management charges and market spread). There is a range of investment objectives.

open interest   The net amount of outstanding OPEN POSITIONS either LONG or SHORT in a given FUTURES or OPTIONS CONTRACT.

open outcry   A public auction system used for FUTURES trading on the floors of futures exchanges where communication is by way of shouting and hand signs between traders.

open position   1. An expression used in FUTURES trading which refers to a LONG or SHORT position which has not been offset by an equal and opposite position. This would make a trader vulnerable to market swings. **2.** A position held by a securities dealer in which purchases or sales have been made which respectively are unsold or not covered. The dealer would be exposed to market swings.

opening purchase   A transaction where a buyer becomes the HOLDER of an OPTION.

opening sale   A transaction where the seller of an OPTION becomes the WRITER.

operating costs   Also known as overheads, these are the costs to a company manufacturing a product or providing services which are additional to the direct costs. Examples of operating costs are administration staff and sales staff salaries, motor vehicles and building costs such as electricity and rates etc. Examples of direct costs are production staff wages and costs of materials.

operating profit   A company's profit after deducting its OPERATING COSTS from GROSS PROFIT.

option   An option gives its HOLDER the right but not the obligation to purchase (CALL OPTION) or sell (PUT OPTION) an instrument such as a commodity or a SECURITY at a specified price on or before a given date.

ordinary shares [UK]   In the UK, the most common form of shares where holders are owners in a company. Ordinary shareholders may share in the company's profits by way of a DIVIDEND if the directors approve such a payout. However it may be that all profits are reinvested in the company so that no dividend is paid. Also dividends may not be payable due to poor results. Holders of ordinary shares will seek to enlarge the capital value of their investment by way of share price increase over the long term. They can also vote on major issues but they are the last in line to be paid in the event of the company being wound up. Similar to common stock in the USA.

organised securities exchange [USA]   A stock exchange where trading of listed securities takes place, such as the NEW YORK STOCK EXCHANGE, as opposed to OVER THE COUNTER trading.

out of the money   1. Either a CALL OPTION where the EXERCISE PRICE is above the current price of the UNDERLYING INSTRUMENT or a PUT OPTION where the exercise price is below the current price of the underlying instrument. **2.** WARRANTS with an exercise price above the market price.

output tax [UK]   The amount of VALUE ADDED TAX (VAT) a company adds to the price of its product or service. After deducting INPUT TAX, the balance must be paid to HM CUSTOMS AND EXCISE. Currently 17.5%.

over the counter (OTC)   The way in which securities are traded by telephone and computer link and not on a listed exchange. Although in the USA the OTC market is regulated by the National Association of Securities Dealers, it is distinctly separate from the NASDAQ Stock Market. OTC securities are those not listed on Nasdaq nor any of the national US securities exchanges.

overbought   A term describing a market in which excessive buying has created an artificially high level. Under these circumstances the market is likely to subsequently fall. See correction.

overcapitalised   A term describing a company which has an excess of capital over what it actually needs. Depending on the ratio between loan capital and share capital, the company will probably be accordingly overloaded with interest and dividend payments.

overdraft   A facility (usually at a bank or other financial institution) enabling an account holder to go into debit for an agreed amount and often for an agreed time. Since money is usually flowing into and out of the account the balance is continually changing and interest is charged on a daily basis. Compared with a loan which is usually for a fixed period with regular repayments, charges tend to be lower for an overdraft. Where a person overdraws without the agreement of the bank, he/she will probably be liable for either heavy charges or in some cases cheques may not be honoured. In principle an overdraft is liable to be recalled at any time.

overheads See operating costs.

oversold A term describing a market in which excessive selling has created an artificially low level. Under these circumstances the market is likely to subsequently rise. See correction.

oversubscribed A term referring to an OFFER FOR SALE where applications for shares exceed the number of shares available. Often applications will be scaled down such that a lower number of shares will be received than those requested.

P

paid in capital   Capital subscribed by shareholders for a company's stock or shares. In the UK, known as paid up capital.

paid up policy   In the USA, a life insurance policy where all premiums have been paid. This may be a policy where premiums are paid for a set number of years after which it is deemed paid up although continuing in force. In the UK, this is cancellation of premiums for a life assurance policy during the policy term where, instead of the policyholder applying for the cash value, he/she elects to leave premiums paid to date as a paid up policy which will give reduced benefits at maturity.

pari passu   Ranking equally. For example, in a new issue of shares which carry equal rights with existing shares they are said to rank pari passu.

par value   The issued price of a security (stocks, shares, bonds etc) which bears no relation to the market price. For example, in the UK, gilts are issued with a par value of £100 and as they are traded on the market throughout their lives their value can vary above or below £100 depending on their popularity at the time. When they reach their REDEMPTION DATE they revert to their par value of £100. Also known as nominal value/nominal price.

partial intestacy   A situation where a WILL does not cover the whole estate of a deceased person.

participating life insurance [USA]   LIFE INSURANCE which pays dividends to policyholders based on the company's investment performance. The policyholder can choose whether to take the dividend in the form of cash, reinvest in the policy or pay a reduced premium.

participating plan [UK]   A WITH PROFITS life assurance policy which participates in the bonuses of the company.

participating preference shares [UK]   PREFERENCE SHARES which, in addition to paying a specified dividend, entitles preference shareholders to participate in receiving an additional dividend if ordinary shareholders are paid a dividend above a stated amount.

participating preferred stock [USA] PREFERRED STOCK which, in addition to paying a specified dividend, entitles preferred stockholders to participate with holders of common stock in receiving any additional dividends.

partly paid shares In PRIVATISATIONS it is usual for shareholders to pay for their shares in two or three instalments. Until the final instalment is made the shares are only partly paid.

partner A person who is a member of a PARTNERSHIP.

partnership Two or more persons working together in the organisation and running of a business. There are two types of partners, that is, general partners and limited partners. General partners are fully responsible for the debts of the business. Limited partners are liable only to the extent of their original investment.

pass book A book of recorded transactions in a savings account, issued by banks in the US and by building societies in the UK in which a customer's deposits, withdrawals and interest are entered. The book is retained by the customer to give an indication of the running balance. See postal account.

passed dividend The failure of a company to pay a scheduled dividend, usually because of reduced profits and often resulting in a reduction of the share price.

pass through security [USA] A security backed by a pool of assets, particularly mortgages, whereby the interest and principal paid on the mortgages is passed through to the shareholder.

pay as you earn (PAYE) [UK] Persons who earn income from employment or who receive a PENSION are liable for income tax under the PAYE system. Taxable pay (gross salary less pension contributions less allowances) is used by the employer to calculate a person's income tax (according to his/her notice of coding) which is passed to the Inland Revenue usually monthly or weekly. This ensures that employees pay their income tax on a regular basis.

pay as you go basis [USA] A system of tax payment by which an employer deducts a proportion of an employees salary for onward remittance to the Inland Revenue Service.

PAYE emergency tax See emergency tax.

payee   A person to whom a payment is made.

payer   A person who makes a payment to a payee.

payment card   A plastic card, either CHARGE CARD, CREDIT CARD or DEBIT CARD used by the owner to purchase goods or services or to obtain cash.

payout ratio [USA]   The proportion of earnings paid out in dividends to shareholders, that is, dividend payment divided by earnings.

pecuniary legacy   See legacy.

P/E ratio   See price/earnings ratio.

penny shares [UK]   Shares with a low value (for example 1p to 20p) traded on a stock exchange. These are often shares in small companies or those which have encountered falling profits and/or problems of debt. Relatively large quantities of shares can be purchased for modest outlays and a price movement upwards by a few pence could result in significant gains. However this type of speculation is considered to be high risk.

penny stocks [USA]   Stocks which normally sell for $1 or less and traded in the OVER THE COUNTER market. They are highly speculative since a relatively small increase or decrease in price can result in significant gains or losses.

Pension Benefit Guaranty Corporation (PBGC) [USA]   A federal corporation, set up in conjunction with the Employee Retirement Income Security Act (ERISA) of 1974, to guarantee basic benefits to participants in pension plans which are underfunded.

pension forecast [UK]   Upon request, a written forecast may be obtained from the BENEFITS AGENCY of the Department of Social Security outlining a person's estimated entitlement to the NATIONAL INSURANCE PENSION (State Pension) at retirement age (Form BR19). It is based on certain assumptions and total NI contributions paid over the person's working life to date. The forecast takes into account the entitlements to the various segments of the National Insurance Pension namely NI BASIC PENSION, STATE EARNINGS RELATED PENSION SCHEME and the GRADUATED RETIREMENT BENEFIT.

pension fund   The total assets of a pension scheme from which a person's pension is paid.

pension mortgage [UK]   A type of PERSONAL PENSION PLAN which utilises the tax free lump sum entitlement from the pension fund at retirement age to repay a MORTGAGE whilst the remainder is (and must be) used to provide a PENSION. Throughout the mortgage term the borrower pays interest to the lender such as a building society or bank whilst additionally making payments into the pension scheme. Tax relief is allowable on both the interest payments to the lender and on the contributions to the pension scheme which makes this type of plan attractive.

pension plan   Regular payments to a person who has retired from employment. In the USA a defined benefit pension plan is one in which an employee's pension benefit is related to number of years service and final salary with each employer. A defined contributions pension plan is one in which benefits are dependent on contributions to and the growth of the pension fund. AN INDIVIDUAL RETIREMENT ACCOUNT (IRA) is a plan which individuals may arrange for themselves. Persons who are self employed may set up a plan for themselves by way of a KEOGH PENSION PLAN. Savings grow tax deferred until benefits are taken. In the UK there are four main types of pension: NATIONAL INSURANCE (NI) PENSION or State Pension; OCCUPATIONAL PENSION; PERSONAL PENSION ; RETIREMENT ANNUITY CONTRACT. A person's pension, after deduction of allowances is liable for income tax.

Pension Schemes Registry [UK]   The Register of all occupational and personal pension schemes. The main objectives are to obtain and record details of all occupational and personal pension schemes and their predecessors, maintain the Register and keep it up to date and to use it to carry out searches on request by members of the public etc.

Pensions Advisory Service   See OPAS.

Pensions Compensation Board [UK]   An independent body set up on 6th April 1997 which may be able to pay compensation to individuals where money has been taken dishonestly from OCCUPATIONAL PENSION SCHEME funds and the employer is bankrupt.

Pensions Ombudsman   See Ombudsman.

peppercorn rent   A nominal rent intended to demonstrate that a property is LEASEHOLD and not FREEHOLD.

performance bond   A form of guarantee, given by the seller in a contract, that in the event of the terms of the contract not being fulfilled, the buyer will be able to claim compensation in the form of money.

performance fund [USA] A MUTUAL FUND with an objective of capital growth with little or no dividend payments.

performance stock USA] A stock whose price is anticipated to grow at an above average rate but with little or no dividend payments.

periodic payment plan [USA] A plan to build up capital in a MUTUAL FUND by regular investments, typically on a monthly or quarterly basis.

permanent health insurance [UK] In return for regular premiums, PHI provides an income in the event of the policy holder contracting a long term illness or injury. There is no payment on death. Benefits are paid usually after a waiting period of several months or even a year known as the DEFERMENT PERIOD. During the deferment period the employer will often pay the employee's salary. The benefit payable will normally be no greater than 75% of earnings in the year preceding the disability and usually continue to retirement age. This is to encourage persons to return to work in the event of partial or full recovery. If a claim becomes payable, the policy holder will receive payment free of tax during the year the disability occurs. This also applies for the subsequent fiscal year (6th April to 5th April).

permanent interest bearing shares (PIBS) [UK] FIXED INTEREST SECURITIES where the rate of interest is known as the COUPON. They are issued by building societies to enable them to raise capital and are tradable on the Stock Exchange. The yield is relatively high but there is no REDEMPTION DATE. This means that the original investment can only be recouped by selling on the open market which is rather small and therefore PIBS may be difficult to sell. Any profit which is made on a sale is not subject to CAPITAL GAINS TAX although the interest payments are liable to INCOME TAX.

perpetual bond A bond without a maturity date which pays interest indefinitely.

perquisite (perk) A benefit given to an employee in addition to his/her salary such as a company car, pension contributions and free products.

personal accident insurance An insurance policy which, in return for regular premiums, pays a specific sum in the event of death, loss of sight or limbs or other permanent disablement due to an accident.

personal accident and sickness insurance An insurance policy similar to PERSONAL ACCIDENT INSURANCE with the additional benefit of cover against disablement due to sickness.

personal accounts   A company's sales accounts of customers contained in the sales LEDGER and purchase accounts of suppliers contained in the purchase ledger are also known as personal accounts. See ledger.

personal allowance [UK]   An allowance, granted to all UK residents, which is deductible from GROSS INCOME, which together with any other allowances such as MARRIED COUPLE'S ALLOWANCE reduce a person's TAXABLE PAY.

personal equity plan (PEP) [UK]   A plan where persons over the age of 18 could formerly invest into the shares of UK and other EC companies via an approved plan manager or through qualifying UNIT TRUSTS and INVESTMENT TRUSTS and receive both income and capital gains free of tax. Maximum annual investment amounts were £6,000 for a general PEP and £3,000 for a single company PEP. PEPs were discontinued on 6th April 1999 and replaced by INDIVIDUAL SAVINGS ACCOUNTS (ISAs), although those PEPs in existence were allowed to continue to grow with similar tax privileges.

personal exemption [USA]   The amount a person may subtract from PERSONAL INCOME when computing federal and state income tax

personal identification number (PIN)   A set of numbers (usually four) which the owner of a PAYMENT CARD uses when withdrawing cash from an automated teller machine (cash dispenser).

personal income [USA]   A person's total income which includes salary, TRANSFER PAYMENTS, dividend and interest income etc.

Personal Investment Authority (PIA) [UK]   A SELF REGULATING ORGANISATION (SRO) authorised by the FINANCIAL SERVICES AUTHORITY (FSA) for the regulation of the majority of companies conducting investment business with private investors in the financial services market. Investment business regulated by the PIA typically includes:

Life assurance
Personal Pension Plans
Unit Trusts
Personal Equity Plans (PEPs)
Guaranteed Income Bonds
Investment Trust Savings Plans
Offshore Funds
Advice and Dealing in Shares
Management of Investment Portfolios
Broker Funds   *cont.*

Enterprise Investment Schemes advice
Advice and Dealing in Traded Options

If an investor wishes to establish if a particular firm is a member of PIA, he/she may check with the CENTRAL REGISTER or with the firm in question.

personal ledger   A book in which the PERSONAL ACCOUNTS of a company are kept that is, the sales ledger and the purchase ledger. See ledger.

personal loan   Loans available from banks and other financial institutions to private individuals for personal use such as the purchase of a motor vehicle, holiday or similar item. Repayment periods vary typically from one year to five years.

personal pension plan [UK]   A savings scheme with taxation advantages introduced by the government during the latter part of the 1980's to enable the self employed and employees working for companies not operating a group pension scheme to build up a pension fund for retirement. The PPP is a MONEY PURCHASE SCHEME and effectively replaced what was known as a RETIREMENT ANNUITY CONTRACT (RAC), also known as a Section 226 policy, which, unless in force before 30th June1988 is no longer available. Contributions to PPPs receive full tax relief up to maximum given percentages of NET RELEVANT EARNINGS for a range of ages. Life assurance may be purchased with up to 5% of net relevant earnings which will receive full tax relief. This percentage is included within the maximum contributions allowable. An employer may contribute to a person's PPP but this is not obligatory. Also a PPP may be used to contract out of SERPS. Up until July 1997 the fund's income and capital gains were free of tax. Thereafter only capital gains are tax free following the government's budget in which TAX CREDITS to pension funds were abolished. All personal pension plans are money purchase schemes where the growth of funds is dependent solely on levels of contributions, the fund manager's competence in investment strategy and management costs. There are basically three types of plan that is, WITH PROFITS, UNIT LINKED and cash funds. Retirement can be taken between the ages of 50 and 75 although it is not necessary to stop working. At retirement up to 25% of the pension fund can be taken as a tax free lump sum with the balance being used to purchase an ANNUITY (the pension). Alternatively, following the Finance Act 1995, the buying of an annuity with the fund balance can be deferred whilst drawing an income from it roughly equivalent to what would have been received from an annuity. This is known as income drawdown (also flexible pension, deferred income etc) which gives flexibility over when the annuity is purchased. However an annuity must be purchased by the age of 75. Both the income drawdown and annuity pension are taxed as earned income, so the recipient is paid net of tax. See phased retirement.

personal possessions   The personal possessions of a deceased person which pass to the BENEFICIARY or beneficiaries of the RESIDUE OF ESTATE unless otherwise stated in the WILL.

petty cash   Cash held by a company on its premises to cover small items of expense. A record of such transactions is usually kept in a petty cash book.

phased retirement [UK]   The arrangement of a PERSONAL PENSION PLAN in segments to enable the policy holder to take a pension in stages. The lump sum entitlement is also phased. The policy holder may elect to phase the purchase of an annuity or to phase income drawdown (see personal pension plan).

physicals   See actuals.

physical delivery   The settlement of a FUTURES contract by receipt or delivery of a COMMODITY

PIA Ombudsman   See Ombudsman.

PIN number   See personal identification number.

pit   An area within a FUTURES exchange where trading in a particular futures or OPTIONS CONTRACT is conducted by OPEN OUTCRY.

place (placing)   The sale of a company's shares to chosen institutions. This can enable a company to join the stockmarket or raise further capital for a LISTED COMPANY.

polarisation [UK]   The distinguishing between INDEPENDENT FINANCIAL ADVISERS who are free to recommend products (life assurance, personal pensions and unit trusts) from a range of companies and COMPANY REPRESENTATIVES (TIED AGENTS) who may only sell the products of one company. In either case a BUYERS GUIDE must be given to the client at the initial interview.

policy document   The document which forms the contract between the insured, that is, the person taking out insurance and the insurer (the insurance company).

policy loan [USA]   The amount a life insurance policyholder may borrow against the CASH SURRENDER VALUE. Interest is payable on the loan which may be deducted from the cash surrender value. In the event of the death of the policyholder any loan outstanding plus interest is deductible from the death benefit. **[UK]** A loan granted by a life assurance company to a policyholder. The extent of the loan is based on a percentage of the surrender value (typically up to 90%) of a WHOLE LIFE or ENDOWMENT POLICY.

poll tax   See community charge.

portability [USA]   The capability of a pension plan holder to transfer pension benefits when changing employment.

portfolio   A schedule of the investments of an institution or individual. In the case of an institution, such as a MUTUAL FUND or UNIT TRUST, investing for say capital growth, details would typically list the range of companies and the holding in each as a percentage of the trust total. For an individual, the portfolio would typically list holdings in equities, bonds, mutual funds, unit trusts, investment trusts and bank deposits etc.

postal account   In the UK, a BUILDING SOCIETY account in which all transactions are conducted via post. In some cases a PASS BOOK is used to record deposits and withdrawals although societies are increasingly acknowledging each of their customer's transactions with a single statement sheet which depicts the amount deposited or withdrawn and the resulting account balance. Also investors now have to produce proof of identity for security reasons prior to the setting up of the account. Interest is payable usually on a six monthly or annual basis and access to funds varies from instant to several months depending on the interest rate being paid, that is, the higher the rate the longer the access time. Interest is paid net of lower rate tax (currently 20%) but non tax payers can elect to have interest paid gross.

Post Office Savings   See National Savings.

postdated check (cheque)   A check with a future date entered. Funds cannot be transferred until that date is reached.

posting   The recording of an entry in a ledger

potentially exempt transfer (PET) [UK]   A gift from one person to another person or body which is not liable to inheritance tax provided the person making the gift lives for at least seven years after the transfer is made. Should death occur before seven years tax will become payable, the amount being related to the number of years following the transfer prior to death according to the table below.

Time from transfer of gift to death	percentage of inheritance tax payable
up to 3 years	100%
3 to 4 years	80%
4 to 5 years	60%
5 to 6 years	40%
6 to 7 years	20%

Any tax which becomes payable is normally charged to the recipient of the gift but in certain circumstances the liability may revert to the donor.

pound cost averaging   In the UK, the regular investing of fixed amounts over regular periods, typically monthly, in order to accumulate holdings in securities such as shares, unit trusts and investment trusts. When for example a unit trust price or investment trust price has fallen then more units or shares will be purchased for that month. Similarly when the price rises then fewer units or shares will be purchased. Over a period of a few years, the average price paid will be lower than the average share price for that period since more shares are bought at the lower price and fewer at the higher price. Similar to dollar cost averaging or constant dollar plan in the USA.

power of attorney   A document which authorises a person to act on behalf of another.

pre tax profit   See profit before tax.

precious metals   The metals gold, silver and platinum. In the UK, gold and silver are traded on the LONDON BULLION MARKET.

preference shares [UK]   The shares of a company, which pay a fixed dividend and which may have a REDEMPTION DATE (the date when the original investment is repaid) at a fixed or variable time in the future. They carry no voting rights unless dividends are in arrears. ORDINARY SHARES carry voting rights and pay dividends in relation to the company's profits which could be generous when profits are high but poor or even non existent in bad times. Preference shares receive dividends before ordinary shares and in the event of the winding up of a company rank higher for repayment.

preferential form   Companies listed on the LONDON STOCK EXCHANGE offering shares to the public are allowed to set aside up to 10% of the issue for application from employees and from shareholders of a parent company floating a subsidiary via a preferential form.

preferred stock [USA]   Stock which pays a fixed dividend and which carries preference over common stock both for dividend payment and claim on assets in the event of liquidation. This type of stock does not normally carry voting rights. Most preferred stock is cumulative (CUMULATIVE PREFERRED STOCK) which means that in the event of a dividend being passed, that is, not paid, it accumulates and must subsequently be paid before the dividends of common stock.

premium   **1.** A lump sum or regular payment in return for a contract of INSURANCE   **2.** When the market price of a NEW ISSUE of shares is higher than the ISSUE PRICE the difference is known as the premium. **3.** When the share price of an INVESTMENT TRUST is higher than its NET ASSET VALUE per share, the shares are said to trade at a premium. **4.** The purchase price of an OPTION. **5.** The amount paid by an investor over the current share price by purchasing shares via the WARRANTS. This is the amount by which the EXERCISE PRICE(2) plus the warrant price exceeds the share price

premium bonds   See National Savings.

prepayment fee   In the US, a fee charged to a borrower by a lender when a loan or mortgage is repaid ahead of schedule. In the UK, building societies impose a similar charge, typically binding the borrower to at least three years of repayments if such a charge is to be avoided.

price   The cost of purchasing a security (shares, bonds etc.).

price earnings ratio (P/E ratio)   A company's share price divided by its EARNINGS PER SHARE.

For example:
Share price = $15   Earnings per Share = $1.50
Price Earnings ratio = $15/$1.50 = 10

A company's P/E ratio shows how high its shares are priced in relation to its earnings. It can also be used as a guide to compare with other companies in the same SECTOR. If the sector average is say 14 and the company in question has a P/E ratio of 10, it could be seen as being relatively sluggish in growth prospects. If another company in the same sector has a P/E ratio of 18 it could indicate a growth company and thus its shares are in demand, so pushing up the share price.

primary market   A market in which NEW ISSUES are traded. A secondary market is a market in which trading of existing securities takes place.

prime rate [USA]   The interest rate which banks offer to their prime customers, that is, those with the most creditworthy records. The UK equivalent is BASE RATE.

principal   **1.** A person or company for whom an AGENT acts. **2.** The FACE VALUE of a debt instrument such as a bond or a note.

prior charges   The fixed liabilities of an INVESTMENT TRUST including LOAN CAPITAL and usually PREFERENCE SHARES. The subtraction of these charges from total assets gives the NET ASSET VALUE of the trust. Prior charges may be expressed either at PAR VALUE or current MARKET VALUE.

prior preferred stock [USA]   Preferred stock with priority over other issues of preferred stock for the payment of dividends and in the event of liquidation.

private company [UK]   A company which is not a PUBLIC LIMITED COMPANY (PLC). It may be a LIMITED COMPANY or unlimited. Private limited companies may not offer shares to the public but may do so to their staff.

private medical insurance   An insurance policy which provides cover in respect of the cost of private medical treatment. This typically includes such items as the fees of consultants, surgeons and anaesthetists, costs of operating theatres and hospital rooms, X-rays, radiotherapy, chemotherapy, drugs and dressings etc.

privatisation   The transferring of ownership of publicly owned or nationalised companies (that is, state controlled companies) to the private sector. This is accomplished via an OFFER FOR SALE.

pro forma invoice   An invoice presented by one company to another for payment for goods prior to their despatch. This method of invoicing is to ensure payment is received and is often the case when two companies have not traded before. If future trading is anticipated it will then be usual for an account to be set up for the purchasing company with credit facilities.

probate   The legal procedure by which a will is authenticated and which confirms the authority of the executors to administer its contents.

profit and loss statement (P&L)   A set of accounts, usually prepared annually, which depict a company's trading performance and normally read in conjunction with the BALANCE SHEET and CASH FLOW data. The profit and loss account can broadly be shown as follows:

Turnover (sales) less manufacturing costs (or cost of sales if for example a retailing company) = gross profit or loss

Gross profit plus any non trading income (for example sale of vehicles) less OPERATING COSTS = operating profit

Operating profit less interest payments to banks or loan stock = net profit before tax (pre tax profit)

Net profit less tax = net profit after tax

Part of the net profit after tax may be used to pay a DIVIDEND with the balance being retained within the business for future investment.

profit before tax   A company's net profit before deduction of CORPORATION TAX.

profit sharing scheme   A scheme where part of a company's profits are paid to employees as an incentive for loyalty and application to the job. The reward may be given via cash, shares or a combination of both.

profit taking   The selling of SECURITIES (for example, shares) when the price has risen in order to lock in to profits.

promissory note   A signed statement promising to pay to a specified person or the bearer a particular sum of money on a fixed date or on demand.

proof of title   In the UK, when a claimant makes a claim in respect of LIFE ASSURANCE, he/she will have to provide evidence of identity and that he/she is entitled to the proceeds, invariably by submitting the policy document. In the event of a claim following the death of the LIFE ASSURED, the death certificate will also need to be submitted to the insurers by the legal representatives of the deceased.

property   An item which is owned, for example a motor car, furniture, paintings, tools etc. These are known as personal property. Buildings and land are known as real property. See property bond.

property bond   A bond issued by LIFE INSURANCE companies to investors whose premiums are invested in property.

property income taxation   See income from property.

property tax [USA]   A tax charged on real property and assessed by consideration to its use. For example whether the land is used for residential, commercial or industrial purposes. In the UK a form of property tax is the COUNCIL TAX.

proposal form A form which is completed by a person applying for a life policy and which forms the basis of the contract.

ProShare   An independent non profit making company with all party support originally set up in 1992 with funding from the government, the London Stock Exchange and 22 companies to encourage wider share ownership for private individuals and employees. It is currently funded by charitable donations from over 100 member companies and by grants from the London Stock Exchange, the Gatsby Trust and Sir John Templeton. ProShare seeks to make share investing more accessible to everyone and to promote the advantages of share ownership as an integral part of long term savings and investment. Its objectives are achieved by media comment via radio, television and the press and by making available a range of literature.

prospect A person who is not currently a client or customer who may (or may not) purchase a product from the seller. If such a person subsequently does buy, he/she becomes a client.

prospectus   A document which sets out a company's financial history, performance, CAPITAL STRUCTURE and future prospects, when shares or other securities are offered for sale to the public.

protected rights [UK]   Pension benefits payable at retirement age which are derived from funds built from minimum contributions paid into an APPROPRIATE PERSONAL PENSION PLAN by the DSS. These benefits are a substitute for part of SERPS.

proxy   A person who acts on behalf of a member of a company for the purpose of voting at a company meeting.

prudential supervision [UK]   A term sometimes used to describe the supervision/regulation of institutions such as banks, building societies and friendly societies where the supervising authority seeks to ensure that the protection of depositors is maintained by the institution in question being financially sound.

public limited company (plc)   A company registered as a public company and which must display the letters plc after its name. Its shares may be offered to the public.

public offering   An offering of new securities to the public. Sometimes known as public issue.

Public Sector Borrowing Requirement (PSBR)   See Public Sector Net Cash Requirement (PSNCR).

Public Sector Net Cash Requirement (PSNCR) [UK]   Formerly known as Public Sector Borrowing Requirement (PSBR), PSNCR is the difference between the expenditure of the public sector and its income. Where there is a deficit it is financed by borrowing, that is, principally via the sale of government gilt edged stocks (gilts). Public sector net borrowing also measures the difference between the expenditure and income of the public sector but differs from the net cash requirement in that it is measured on an accruals basis whereas the net cash requirement is mainly a cash measure.

purchased life annuity   See annuity.

purchase ledger   See ledger.

purchasing power [USA]   The amount of goods and services which can be purchased by a dollar after taking into account the effect of inflation. Purchasing power can be assessed by tracking an index of consumer prices and comparing different periods, for example the early 1990s and the current time. Inflation will result in reduced purchasing power over a period of time.

pure endowment [UK]   A LIFE ASSURANCE policy where the SUM ASSURED is paid if the LIFE ASSURED survives the term but in the event of prior death nothing is payable.

put option   An OPTION which gives the HOLDER the right but not the obligation to sell a stated quantity of the UNDERLYING INSTRUMENT (for example, shares, indices, commodities, etc.) at a specified price on or before a given date.

Q

qualification period [USA] That period of time, as stated in an insurance policy, during which benefits are not payable to the insured following a claim. This period is to enable the insurance company to confirm that the claim is genuine and is usual in health insurance.

qualified plan [USA] A TAX DEFERRED pension plan set up by an employer to enable employees to accumulate tax free savings for retirement benefits. Usually, contributions are made by employer and employee and when income is taken at retirement it is taxable.

qualified stock option [USA] A STOCK OPTION, given to executives and employees, which complies with the requirements of the Internal Revenue Service. A qualified stock option is not subject to tax at the grant date or when exercised.

qualifying annuity [USA] An ANNUITY which is purchased within a QUALIFIED PLAN.

qualifying policy [UK] The proceeds from a LIFE ASSURANCE policy to an individual are free of tax provided the policy is qualifying. The rules which govern qualification are: a) The premiums must be payable for ten years or 75% of the term whichever is the shorter. For example a ten year endowment plan will qualify after seven and a half years. b) The premiums must be paid regularly on an annual or more frequent basis such as monthly. c) The sum assured must be at least 75% of the total premiums payable over the life of the policy. Additionally, if the policy was in force before 14th March 1984, tax relief can be claimed on the premiums (known as LIFE ASSURANCE PREMIUM RELIEF).

quartile UNIT TRUSTS or INVESTMENT TRUSTS within given SECTORS may be ranked to compare their performance. Each sector is divided into four groups by descending order of performance with each group being known respectively as 1st, 2nd, 3rd and 4th quartiles. For example if a sector contains thirty six trusts, each quartile will contain nine trusts. Trusts will often advertise their performance over various periods (for example,one, three, five and ten years) by indicating, say, a first quartile ranking which in the above case would indicate a position in the top nine.

quotation   The highest bid price and the lowest offer price of a security available at a particular time.

quoted company   See listed company.

quoted price   The price of a SECURITY or COMMODITY.

R

raider An individual or organisation who seeks to take over a company by purchasing its shares.

random walk The theory that share price movements are not linked in any way to their past history. This is in complete contrast to charting where CHARTISTS predict future trends based on past movement.

rating [USA] The classification of the quality of bonds by various rating services. A bond with the highest rating is classified as AAA. See bond rating.

real account A LEDGER account detailing assets and capital (such as buildings and machinery).

real estate Property comprising land and buildings, fences etc as opposed to personal property. Also known as real property.

real estate agent [USA] An agent engaged by a real estate broker.

real estate broker [USA] One who arranges the sale and purchase of property in return for a commission. Known as an estate agent in the UK.

real estate investment trust (REIT) [USA] A publicly traded investment trust which invests the capital of its shareholders in a variety of real estate.

real property See real estate.

real time A reference made to actual time in a computer process. For example a company selling a product in varying volume and using a computer real time process would be able to establish from any of its terminals the balance of stock immediately after any sales through any of those terminals.

receiver A person appointed by a court to wind up the affairs of a company and to utilise assets to pay its CREDITORS.

recession   A decrease in GROSS NATIONAL PRODUCT (GNP) for two consecutive quarters. A severe recession is known as a DEPRESSION or slump.

Recognised Clearing House [UK]   A CLEARING HOUSE which meets the requirements for recognition under the FINANCIAL SERVICES ACT 1986 and approved by the FINANCIAL SERVICES AUTHORITY (FSA).

Recognised Investment Exchange [UK]   An INVESTMENT exchange which meets the requirements for recognition under the FINANCIAL SERVICES ACT 1986 and approved by the FINANCIAL SERVICES AUTHORITY (FSA).

Recognised Professional Body [UK]   A body which regulates the practice of a profession such as the Institute of Chartered Accountants, The Law Society, the Institute of Actuaries and the Insurance Brokers' Registration Council. Companies which are members of such bodies may be authorised by their RPB to conduct investment business via powers delegated by the FINANCIAL SERVICES AUTHORITY (FSA). Those companies may currently conduct investment business up to a limit of 20% of their income from their main practice.

recovery stocks/shares   Shares which have decreased in value but are considered to be capable of recovering to their former price.

redeemable   Something which can be bought back by the original issuer from the purchaser.

redeemable preference shares   PREFERENCE SHARES which the issuing company reserves the right to redeem. The shares may, or may not have a specific REDEMPTION DATE or dates.

redemption   The re-purchase of a DEBT SECURITY such as a bond, or PREFERRED STOCK by the issuing company at or before maturity.

redemption date   The actual date on which repayment of a BOND or LOAN STOCK takes place.

redemption fees [USA]   Fees imposed by a MUTUAL FUND on shareholders who dispose of shares within a relatively short period after purchase.

redemption price [USA]   The price at which a BOND or PREFERRED STOCK can be redeemed by the issuer.

redemption yield   See yield.

refer to drawer   A phrase used by banks in the UK when a cheque is dishonoured or 'bounced'.

registered securities   Shares and bonds etc where holders have their names kept in a register maintained by the issuing company.

registrar   **1.**   A person with responsibility for keeping a register of records and transactions.   **2.**   An organisation with responsibility for keeping a register of bonds and stock issues.

Registrar of Companies   The official body with responsibility for the registration of all companies in the UK.

reimbursement   The repayment of a person who has incurred expenses on behalf of another. For example the reimbursement of an employee who has paid money on business related expenses (such as travel expenses) on behalf of his/her employer.

reinsurance   The covering of all or some of an insurance risk by an insurer by transferring to another insurer in return for the payment or part payment of premiums.

reinvestment of dividends   Instead of a cash dividend being paid to a shareholder, the dividend amount is used to purchase more shares.

remortgage   The arranging of alternative finance for the purchase of a property which is already mortgaged. For example obtaining a mortgage with a lower interest rate to replace the existing mortgage.

renewable term life insurance [USA] renewable term assurance [UK]   Term life insurance with a term for example of three years, at the end of which the policy can be renewed for a further three years and similarly thereafter for an overall specified length of time.

renounceable documents   Documents which provide temporary evidence of ownership of unregistered shares. These include a company's offer of shares to the public, a RIGHTS ISSUE and a capitalisation or SCRIP ISSUE. In each case instructions are given regarding action to be taken if the holder requires to have the shares registered in his/her name or if it is required to renounce them in favour of another person.

rent   Regular payment by a TENANT to an owner for the use of his/her land or buildings.

renunciation   The relinquishing of shares by one person to another by the completion of a renunciation form usually attached to the ALLOTMENT LETTER.

repayment mortgage   A MORTGAGE where throughout the TERM, regular payments (usually monthly) are made to partly repay interest on the capital and to partly repay the capital itself (the amount of the loan). Initially the large proportion of the repayments will be used to pay interest since the capital amount outstanding is at its highest value. Therefore over the initial years the capital will not reduce very much. However as the years proceed more and more of the monthly repayments will be applied to reducing the capital until towards the end of the term the large proportion will be paying off capital and a small proportion paying interest. In the event that interest rates rise then often the monthly repayments will rise accordingly. Alternatively to keep the same monthly repayments the term will need to be extended. If interest rates fall then the reverse applies. It is usually a requirement of the lender (that is, a building society or bank) providing the mortgage that the borrower takes out LIFE ASSURANCE so that repayment is made in the event of his/her death during the term.

reserves   Mainly the retained profits of a company and forming part of its CAPITAL.

residence status [UK]   The definition of a person's status when living or working outside the UK with regard to his/her taxation liabilities. This can be:

1) Resident in the UK.   This applies if:
More than 183 days are spent in the UK in the tax year.
The UK is visited on a continuing basis where the average visiting time is over 3 months taken over 4 consecutive years.
The person is a British or Irish subject who is ordinarily resident in the UK and occasionally resident abroad.

2) Ordinarily Resident in the UK.   This applies if:
The person resides in the UK on a permanent basis.

3) Domiciled in the UK.   There are a number of types of domicile, that is, domicile of origin, domicile of dependence and domicile of choice. This is a very complicated aspect of general law and advice should be sought when dealing with these matters.

residuary estate   The remainder of an estate after the payment of debts, expenses and taxes and the distribution of LEGACIES. Also known as residue of estate in the UK.

residuary legacy   See legacy.

resistance level   Price levels at which shares stop rising. See support level.

retail investor   US term for an investor who buys securities on his/her behalf through a stockbroker.

retail price index (RPI)   An index of the prices of goods in retail outlets used to measure the rate of INFLATION.

retailer card   A plastic PAYMENT CARD issued by a specific retailer or group of retailers for limited use at their own outlets.

retained earnings   That proportion of a company's profits after tax, not paid in dividends but reinvested in the CAPITAL of the company.

retirement   The termination of employment at which time salary is substituted by a pension.

retirement annuity contract [UK]   Prior to 30th June1988, persons not in pensionable employment (employment where no pension scheme exists) or persons who were self employed were able to qualify for tax relief for contributions made to a pension scheme known as a retirement annuity under section s226 of the Income and Corporation Taxes Act 1970. Although RACs were replaced by PERSONAL PENSION PLANS from 1st July 1988 those already in force may continue to operate.

retirement pension forecast   See pension forecast.

return on investment   The overall profit (or loss) expressed as a percentage of the original investment.

For example:
A person invests $5,000 in the shares of a company and some time later has received £100 in dividends with the value of the shares now $5,200. Return on investment will be:
[($100 + $5,200 - $5,000)/$5,000] x 100 = ($300/$5,000) x 100 = 6%.

revenue account   An INVESTMENT TRUST term referring to analysis of investment income. This details whether income is FRANKED or unfranked and whether the source of income is from UK investments, overseas or unlisted securities.

reverse annuity mortgage (RAM) [USA]   A mortgage that permits a normally elderly person or persons who own their home outright to receive an income for life in return for gradually relinquishing ownership in the property.

reverse mortgage [USA]   A mortgage that permits a normally elderly person or persons who own their home outright to receive an income with the home as collateral. The loan is repaid plus interest either at the end of the term or on the death of the borrower when the property would be sold.

reverse leverage [USA]   The investment of borrowed money where the return fails to match the interest payable on the loan.

reversionary bonus [UK]   A bonus added to the SUM ASSURED (or BASIC SUM ASSURED) of a WITH PROFITS life assurance policy out of a life company's surplus profits usually on an annual basis. These bonuses are payable at the end of the TERM of the policy (that is, at MATURITY) or on prior death of the LIFE ASSURED and once allocated, their values are guaranteed provided premiums are paid up to maturity or death. The values of such bonuses are usually related to the sum assured and can be either simple reversionary bonuses (related to the sum assured only) or compound reversionary bonuses (related to the sum assured plus bonuses to date). Reversionary bonuses may sometimes be taken in cash at the time they are declared but the values will be significantly lower compared with leaving them until maturity. See terminal bonus.

right of redemption [USA]   The right to recover property forfeited by FORECLOSURE by paying the outstanding principal owed plus interest.

right of survivorship   The right of a joint owner to full title of a property when the death of the other joint owner occurs.

rights issue   An invitation by a LISTED FIRM or LISTED COMPANY to its shareholders to purchase additional shares to enable it to raise new capital. The offer is usually to purchase a quantity of new shares in proportion to those already owned and at a discount to the current market price. For example in a one for five rights issue, a shareholder would be invited to buy one new share for every five shares owned. The discount could typically be around 20%.

rights offering   See rights issue.

risk/reward   A term which relates to considering the returns from different types of financial instruments (for example bank deposits, bonds, shares, mutual funds, unit trusts, investment trusts, futures and options etc) whilst bearing in mind the attendant risks. For example a CAPITAL sum deposited with a bank or building society will usually be very safe since it is unlikely that either will fail as a business. The capital, whilst remaining relatively safe will also earn interest. However such interest will be partially devalued by INFLATION and will not normally be particularly competitive over the long term. On the other hand investment in equities (shares, mutual funds, unit trusts, investment trusts etc) will normally over the long term give greater returns but the risk is much higher. Also in the short term they could easily fall in value. Thus investors will usually seek to build a balanced PORTFOLIO of investments to include low risk deposits for safety (bank deposits, bonds) and longer term higher risk instruments such as equities for greater potential growth.

risk capital   See venture capital.

rolling settlement [UK]   Prior to 18th July 1994, purchases and sales of SECURITIES were combined during an ACCOUNT period (normally ten working days) to arrive at a net settlement figure which was due for payment on the second Monday following that account period. After 18th July 1994, a rolling settlement was introduced which initially commenced on a ten day basis (known as T+10) whereby settlement was due ten days after dealing. This was subsequently reduced to five days (T+5). The purpose of these and other changes was to reduce the settlement periods and generally speed up transactions. See CREST.

rollover   **1.** The transferring of funds from one investment to another such as rolling over the proceeds from a bond which has matured into another bond. **2.** The term used when a borrower obtains authority from a bank to delay a principal payment on a loan. **3.** The movement of a FUTURES or OPTIONS position from one delivery/expiry month to a further dated month by trading out of the existing position and simultaneously trading into the further dated month.

round lot [USA]   The normal TRADING UNIT on a securities exchange. A round lot on the New York Stock Exchange is 100 for shares and $1,000 face value for a bond.

round trip   The opening purchase or sale of a FUTURES or OPTIONS CONTRACT and the subsequent opposite and closing sale or purchase in the same contract. It is usual for transaction costs to be quoted on a round trip basis.

Royal Mint   The organisation in the UK, located in Llantrisant and responsible to the Chancellor of the Exchequer, which possesses the sole right to manufacture coins and notes of the realm.

rule of 72   An arithmetic equation using compound annual interest rate and number of years of investment to enable the *doubling* of an investment to be roughly estimated. The number 72 is divided by the period known to find the annual compound interest required. Similarly the number 72 is divided by the compound interest rate to find the period required. For example, if a person wishes to double his/her investment over a period of 10 years and requires to know what compound annual interest would be necessary to achieve this growth, then 72/10 = 7.2 that is, approximately 7%.

S

salary reduction plan [USA] A TAX DEFERRED retirement plan which provides for an employee to have a certain amount of gross salary withheld and invested in a choice of stocks and bonds. Contributions and fund growth are free of tax until withdrawal.

sales ledger See ledger.

sales charge A brokerage fee charged to a buyer of shares in a MUTUAL FUND. The charge is deducted prior to the balance being invested in the fund.

sales tax [USA] A state or local government tax levied on goods and services. The amount of tax is based on a percentage of the selling price. An item costing $100 and a sales tax of 5% will cost in total $105.

save as you earn (SAYE) [UK] A former government scheme which allowed tax concessions to persons making regular savings from their salaries into certain building society, bank and NATIONAL SAVINGS accounts. Maximum savings per month were £20 and tax free bonuses paid after five and seven years. SAYE was abolished after the November 1994 Budget.

savings account An account with a bank or financial institution where savings are made. Interest is paid usually once or twice per year and will be relative to the amount of money in the account and current interest rates. There is often a notice period required for withdrawals and the longer this term the higher the interest rate. In the USA savings accounts are insured up to $100,000 at banks insured by the Federal Deposit Insurance Corporation. In the UK, compensation up to a maximum of £18,000 is payable where an authorised bank or building society fails. See DEPOSIT PROTECTION SCHEME. See BUILDING SOCIETIES INVESTOR PROTECTION SCHEME.

savings and loan association [USA] A financial institution in which depositors' savings are used to provide home mortgages loans.

savings element [USA] The cash value which accumulates within a life insurance policy. The premium is applied to give both life cover plus a savings element which is allowed to grow tax deferred until withdrawn.

schedule   That part of an INSURANCE or ASSURANCE policy which sets out the particular details relevant to a contract. Details which are listed are typically the policy name and number, the policyholder's name, the commencement and maturity dates, the benefits payable, the life or lives assured in the case of life assurance and the premiums payable etc.

Schedule A, B, C, D, E, F   See Taxation Schedules.

scrip dividend [UK]   The issue of additional shares by a company to a shareholder equivalent to the cash value of the dividend if he/she chooses this method of payment.

scrip issue   The issuing of additional shares by a company to its shareholders in proportion to their existing holdings but resulting in a correspondingly lower market price. This is achieved by the company by transferring funds from reserves into capital. For example: A person owns 1000 shares with a current price of £6 per share. If the company makes a 2 for 1 scrip issue (that is, for every share owned two further shares will be issued) the shareholder will now own 3000 shares but the price will adjust to £2 per share and the overall value will remain at £6000. The main purpose of this exercise is to make the shares more marketable in that there will be a lot more in circulation and the price more attractive at the lower level.

SEAQ International   The London Stock Exchange's electronic price quotation system for non UK securities.

seasoned issue   A security issued by a well established and sound performing company with generally high LIQUIDITY.

seat   A membership on a securities or commodities exchange.

second hand endowment   See traded endowment policy.

second mortgage   The taking out of a MORTGAGE on a property which is already mortgaged. This can be used to raise capital if the property has significantly increased in value and would involve finance companies rather than banks or building societies. Since the first mortagee (lender) usually holds the deeds of the property, the second mortgagee will carry a higher risk and thus charges a considerably higher rate of interest

secondary market   A market in which trading of existing securities takes place.(for example on a stock exchange). Also traded on a stock exchange are NEW ISSUES that is, a PRIMARY MARKET.

section

Section 32 transfer [UK]   A reference to section 32 of the Finance Act 1981 which defined the original legislation allowing a person to transfer a payment representing pension benefits from a previous employer (that is, from an OCCUPATIONAL PENSION SCHEME) to a PERSONAL PENSION PLAN operated by an insurance company (with approved pension schemes) of the person's choice.

Section 226 policy   See retirement annuity contract (RAC).

Section 352 of the Income and Corporation Taxes Act 1988   See certificate of deduction of tax.

sector   A group of companies with similar products or services which is listed with financial information such as share prices and yield etc. This information is published in the national press. For example reference to the chemicals sector in a financial newspaper enables share price performance of companies engaged in chemical products and services to be compared.

sector fund   A MUTUAL FUND or UNIT TRUST which invests in a specific SECTOR such as chemicals or telecommunications.

secured bond   A bond which is secured by the guarantee of assets or collateral.

secured loan   A loan where the borrower offers an asset to which the lender has access in the event of the borrower failing to make the loan repayments.

secured creditor   A CREDITOR who has a charge over the assets of a DEBTOR in the event of the debtor failing to meet his/her obligations.

Securities and Exchange Commission (SEC) [USA]   A federal agency empowered to regulate US financial markets in order to protect investors against fraudulent dealings by way of full public DISCLOSURE.

Securities and Futures Authority (SFA) [UK]   A SELF REGULATING ORGANISATION (SRO) with responsibility for the regulation of firms engaged in the securities and futures sectors of the financial services market. Companies regulated by the SFA are those engaged in dealing or advising in SECURITIES or DERIVATIVES including SHARES, BONDS, TRADED OPTIONS, corporate finance and FUTURES. A list of authorised firms is published from time to time by the SFA enabling clients to confirm authenticity.

Securities and Investments Board (SIB) [UK]   A private limited company formerly reporting to the Chancellor of the Exchequer with responsibility for the regulation of the UK investment market in accordance with the Financial Services Act 1986. It was replaced by the FINANCIAL SERVICES AUTHORITY (FSA) in October 1997.

Securities Investor Protection Corporation (SIPC) [USA]   A non profit organization which provides insurance for cash and securities in customer accounts held by approved brokerage firms. Brokers and dealers registered with the SECURITIES AND EXCHANGE COMMISSION are obliged to be members of SIPC. In the event that such a firm fails, investors are covered up to a maximum of $500,000 of which no more than $100,000 can be cash.

security 1. A financial asset such as a share or bond. **2.** An asset which is offered by a borrower to a lender to safeguard a loan.

segmentation   A number of small identical policies (for example, life insurance or pension policies) rather than a single large policy. Use of this arrangement can be helpful when taking a pension in that it allows PHASED RETIREMENT according to the requirements of the policyholder.

Self Assessment [UK]   From April 1996 all taxpayers in the UK were obliged by law to maintain records of their income of all types and capital gains so as to enable tax returns to be completed. This is known as Self Assessment. Those people who normally complete a tax return must do so together with one or more schedules, the latter being relevant to the individual's particular circumstances - for example employees must complete the schedule for employment income. Upon completion of the returns and schedules, individuals may themselves calculate the tax due or submit them to the Inland Revenue to make the calculations. Alternatively the services and advice of an accountant can be obtained.

Self Regulating Organisation (SRO) [UK]   Following the Financial Services Act 1986, SROs were set up to regulate companies dealing in investment business with the objective of investor protection. There are currently three SROs, the SECURITIES AND FUTURES AUTHORITY (SFA), the PERSONAL INVESTMENT AUTHORITY (PIA) and the INVESTMENT MANAGEMENT REGULATORY ORGANISATION (IMRO) which report to the FINANCIAL SERVICES AUTHORITY (FSA). However, in due course, the regulatory functions of the SROs are scheduled to be acquired by the FSA.

senior debt [USA]   A debt which receives priority for repayment in the event of a corporation's liquidation.

senior mortgage bond [USA] A mortgage bond which receives priority on the assets of a company over other bonds in the event of liquidation.

serial bond A bond which is arranged to be repaid in instalments over a period of time.

series OPTIONS CONTRACTS on the same instrument (for example an index such as the FT-SE 100 Index) having the same EXERCISE PRICE and EXPIRY DATE are known as the same series. PUT OPTIONS and CALL OPTIONS having the same exercise price and expiry date are two different series.

settlement **1.** The payment of monies owed following dealing on a stock exchange. Currently the period allowed is three days after the trade in the US and five days in the UK. See rolling settlement. **2.** The payment of monies owed by one party to another. **3.** The dispersal of property made by deed or will where a trust is set up. The beneficiaries are the persons who gain from the settlement and the person setting up the trust and providing the property for settlement is the SETTLOR.

settlement day The day on which purchased securities are due for delivery to the buyer and payment is due to be made to the seller.

settlement options [USA] The various options available to the beneficiaries of a life insurance policy in the event of the death of the insured. For example a lump sum or an income.

settlor A person who sets up a trust or makes a SETTLEMENT by means of money or property.

share A unit of ownership in a corporation or company, MUTUAL FUND or LIMITED PARTNERSHIP.

share account [UK] A BUILDING SOCIETY account where there is no cheque book facility. Interest is usually variable and sometimes there is a notice period for withdrawals. Share account holders are members of the society and are entitled to vote and attend annual general meetings.

share capital The proportion of a company's capital which derives from the issue of SHARES, the most common being COMMON STOCK and PREFERRED STOCK (USA) and ORDINARY SHARES and PREFERENCE SHARES (UK). See capital structure.

share certificate A certificate denoting ownership of shares in a particular company. The current trend is away from paper certificates towards NOMINEE ACCOUNTS.

share index   An INDEX representing the combination of a number of specified company share values. For example the Dow Jones Industrial Average is the main USA share index which monitors the movement of 30 particular industrial companies traded on the NEW YORK STOCK EXCHANGE. The FT-SE 100 INDEX is a measure of the combined share prices of the 100 largest companies (by MARKET CAPITALISATION) in the UK. Such indices are constantly updated with a view to tracking changes.

share option [UK]   An incentive given to company directors and employees to promote loyalty and commitment. The scheme works by way of the employee being offered shares in the company at a fixed price (at or below the market price) for a specified time, for example five years. The option to purchase may be exercised at any time (or stated times) during this period. If the company is trading profitably and expanding the share price may well increase substantially over the option period thus providing a valuable capital gain for the employee should he/she decide to sell. Tax liabilities may be reduced on gains where schemes are approved by the Inland Revenue. Known as a stock option in the USA.

share price total return   The gain (or loss) on a share price including the reinvestment of dividends into additional shares over a given period of time. The term is often used by INVESTMENT TRUSTS.

shared appreciation mortgage (SAM) [USA]   A mortgage in which a borrower pays a below normal rate of interest to the lender on the understanding that the latter shares a proportion of the appreciation of the property.

shareholder   The owner of shares in a company.

shell company   A company which exists in name only and which has ceased to trade. Such a company can be sold to new owners at a lower cost than setting up a new business.

short   See short position.

short bond [USA]   A bond with a near maturity date, generally under two years.

shorts [UK]   1) REDEEMABLE GILTS or bonds with a redemption date within five years. 2) Securities, commodities or financial instruments held in a SHORT POSITION.

short position   The selling of a security, commodity or financial instrument (for example, currencies etc.) which may not be owned by the seller in the belief that the price will fall. The seller would then hope to buy it back at a lower price and thus make a profit. See long position.

short term debt [USA]   Debts (or current liabilities) falling due within one year.

sickness benefit [UK]   A benefit payable by the state to employed persons who become sick and unable to work for more than three days and are not entitled to STATUTORY SICK PAY (payment by the employer for the first eight weeks of sickness). Where employers pay their employees statutory sick pay, the state benefit becomes applicable if the illness continues beyond the eight week period. The extent of the benefit is dependent on the person's national insurance contributions and the maximum benefit period is 28 weeks. Sickness benefit is not taxable.

sickness insurance   See permanent health insurance. See personal accident and sickness insurance.

simple interest   Interest, normally paid annually, which is earned on deposited capital only, that is, unlike COMPOUND INTEREST, the annual interest is not added to the capital. For example:

> **Year 1:** Original deposit = £1,000.00
> Annual simple interest (paid once per year) = 8%
> At end of year, deposit   = £1,000.00 Simple interest = £80.00
> **Year 2:** Deposit   = £1,000.00
> At end of year, deposit = £1,000.00   Simple interest = £80.00
> **Year 3:** Deposit   = £1,000.00
> At end of year, deposit = £1,000.00 Simple interest = £80.00

Thus after three years the account value is £1,000.00 + £240.00 = £1,240.00.

simple reversionary bonus [UK]   A WITH PROFITS life assurance bonus, normally declared annually, which is based on the profits of the life company's investments. The simple reversionary bonus is calculated on the SUM ASSURED (or BASIC SUM ASSURED) only and is payable at the maturity of the policy or prior death. Once REVERSIONARY BONUSES are declared, they cannot be withdrawn by the life company provided the policy conditions are fulfilled until a claim is made (that is, at maturity or previous death). See compound reversionary bonus.

simplified employee pension plan (SEP) [USA]   A pension plan, set up by an employee, in which both employer and employee contribute to an INDIVIDUAL RETIREMENT ACCOUNT (IRA).

single company PEP [UK]   See personal equity plan (PEP).

single premium life insurance   A single payment for an insurance policy rather than regular premiums.

single premium bond   See investment bond.

slump   A severe RECESSION over a lengthened period.

social security disability income insurance [USA]   Insurance which provides income to disabled persons incapacitated for one year or more. Benefits are payable up to the person's death.

social security tax [USA]   A federal tax imposed on income and paid equally by employer and employee up to a maximum income level.

soft dollars [USA]   Payment to a broker by a customer by way of commission charges for services provided rather than a fee (known as hard dollars).

special bonus [UK]   An additional bonus (that is, over and above the normal REVERSIONARY BONUS) applied to a WITH PROFITS life assurance policy when the life company's profits are exceptional.

specialist [USA]   A member of a stock exchange who provides an orderly market in one or more securities. A specialist executes LIMIT ORDERS and buys and sells securities when abnormal fluctuations occur to maintain stability.

specialised mutual fund [USA]   See sector fund.

specific legacy   See legacy.

speculation   The buying and/or selling of securities, commodities, currencies etc with a view to making relatively quick profits as opposed to long term investment. This type of trading is particularly prevalent in markets such as commodity futures and options.

split [USA]   The issuing of additional shares by a corporation to its shareholders in proportion to their existing holdings but resulting in a correspondingly lower market price and as such no change in the value of the shareholders' equity. In a two for one split, original ownership of 1,000 shares at $10 per share changes to 2,000 shares at $5 per share .

split capital investment trust (split-level trust) [UK]   An INVESTMENT TRUST with a limited life, in which the equity capital is divided into ous classes of income shares and capital shares. Holders of income shares receive the majority of the trust's income throughout its life and a specified capital amount on liquidation. Holders of capital shares receive virtually no income during the trust's life but on liquidation receive all the assets after repayment of capital to holders of income shares. These trusts are becoming more complicated in that they can now provide shares which offer income and capital at different levels of return and risk.

spot Another word for immediate.

spot market A market in the UNDERLYING INSTRUMENT (for example, shares, commodities etc) on which a FUTURES or OPTIONS contract is based. This market is for immediate delivery as opposed to future delivery. Also known as cash market or physical market.

spot price The price of the UNDERLYING INSTRUMENT (for example, shares, commodities etc) in a SPOT MARKET.

spousal IRA [USA] An INDIVIDUAL RETIREMENT ACCOUNT set up on behalf of a non working spouse.

spread The difference between the buying price and selling price of a security.

stag A person who applies for shares in a NEW ISSUE with the intention of selling them soon after trading begins. This is in the hope that the price will have immediately increased to provide a quick profit.

stagflation Economic stagnation (or RECESSION) combined with INFLATION.

stamp duty [UK] A tax imposed on certain transactions which is collected when the legal document confirming the transaction has been stamped. An example of where stamp duty applies in the UK is the transfer of land and property, payable by the purchaser. Currently, transfer of property over a value of £60,000 is subject to 1% stamp duty. Transfer of property over £250,000 carries a charge of 2.5% and property over £500,000 a charge of 3.5%. Stamp duty is also currently payable on the purchase of shares at the rate of 0.5%.

Standard and Poor's Composite Index (S&P 500) An index of the share prices of 500 US companies reflecting the general trend of the US stock market. The index covers the shares of industrial, transport, utilities and financial corporations.

standing order [UK] An order by a customer to his/her banker to pay a specified amount usually on or around a particular day of the month regularly to another account. This could be typically to a person's building society for regular payment of mortgage interest or for premiums for life assurance. If the payee, for example, a building society, requires payments to be increased (or decreased) it must write to the customer requesting a change in the amount of the standing order. The customer then instructs his/her bank accordingly. The current trend for regular payments however seems to be towards DIRECT DEBIT where the customer agrees to the payee debiting (claiming funds from) his/her account.

State Earnings Related Pension Scheme (SERPS) [UK]   A government scheme introduced in April 1978 to provide a PENSION, related to the earnings of employed persons only, in addition to the NI BASIC PENSION. Employees make payments to SERPS and the NI Basic Pension by way of Class 1 NATIONAL INSURANCE (NI) CONTRIBUTIONS. (Employers also pay Class 1 contributions on all the employee's earnings). Employees may elect to contract out of SERPS and pay less Class 1 contributions via a rebate which may be invested in an OCCUPATIONAL PENSION or a PERSONAL PENSION PLAN.

statement See statement of account. See bank statement.

statement of account A document, issued by a supplier to its customer, listing transactions over a given period, normally monthly. It will include details of invoices, payments received and any credits approved with a resultant balance payable by the customer.

statutory sick pay [UK]   Sick pay made by employers to employees when the latter incur an illness or injury and are unable to work for more than three consecutive days. SSP is payable for the first eight weeks of absence after which SICKNESS BENEFIT becomes payable. SSP payments to employees are taxable and employers can reclaim these amounts from the DSS.

stepped interest debenture stocks [UK]   A DEBENTURE stock where the rate of interest payable to lenders is increased in stages over the initial life until a certain rate is reached. Thereafter, the rate remains fixed until the REDEMPTION DATE. This type of debenture is advantageous to an INVESTMENT TRUST in that interest payments will be lower than the norm in the initial years (whilst the trust consolidates its growth) and above the norm in the later years (when it will be expected that the trust's assets can afford the extra interest).

stepped preference shares   PREFERENCE SHARES with dividends which increase annually by a specified amount and with a predetermined capital return.

sterling   The currency of the UK (the UK pound).

stock [USA]   Shares in a corporation conferring ownership on the holder. The two main types of stock are COMMON STOCK and PREFERRED STOCK. Owners of common stock are entitled to vote at shareholder meetings and to receive a dividend if payable. Owners of preferred stock receive an annual dividend before common stockholders and priority in the event of the liquidation of a company. However they do not, as a rule, have voting rights. [UK] Fixed interest securities such as GILTS. There is normally a REDEMPTION DATE when the PAR VALUE is repaid to whoever is the holder at the time. They are traded on stock exchanges where their prices fluctuate according to demand, influencing factors including interest rates and time to redemption.

stock dividend [USA]   The payment of a dividend to shareholders in the form of stock instead of cash. If a company declares a 5% stock dividend, a shareholder with 1,000 shares will receive an additional 50 shares. Known as a SCRIP DIVIDEND in the UK.

stock exchange   A MARKET where SECURITIES are bought and sold. In the USA, the NEW YORK STOCK EXCHANGE is the largest exchange and in the UK, the LONDON STOCK EXCHANGE is the equivalent largest exchange.

Stock Exchange Automated Quotation system (SEAQ)   The computerised system at the LONDON STOCK EXCHANGE which continuously updates prices and trade reports for UK securities (shares, gilts etc). SEAQ lists the MARKET MAKERS' bid and offer prices.

Stock Exchange Daily Official List   See Daily Official List.

Stock Exchange Pool Nominee (SEPON)   The NOMINEE COMPANY where all stocks and shares are held during the course of settlement on the LONDON STOCK EXCHANGE.

stock in trade   Raw materials and finished products carried in stock by a company. These would be included in the company's assets on the BALANCE SHEET.

stock option [USA]   An incentive given to executives and employees to promote loyalty and commitment. The scheme works by way of the employee being offered shares in the company at a fixed price (at or below the market price) for a specified time, for example five years. The option to purchase may be exercised at any time (or stated times) during this period. If the company is trading profitably and expanding, the share price may well increase substantially over the option period thus providing a valuable capital gain for the employee. A QUALIFIED STOCK OPTION is not subject to tax at the grant date or when exercised. See option.

stock symbol An abbreviation of letters allocated to a company by the exchange on which its stock is traded.

stock transfer form The form which the seller of a security (the transferor) signs when transferring his/her holding to a new owner (the transferee), who also signs.

stock warrant [USA] A transferable security often issued with PREFERRED STOCK or a BOND which grants the owner the right to purchase a related quantity of COMMON STOCK at a specific price at a future date. Some warrants do not have a maturity date. No dividends are payable, nor are there voting rights.

stockbroker A BROKER dealing in stocks and shares on behalf of a client. In the UK, after the reorganisation of the stock market in October 1986, (known as BIG BANG) many stockbrokers have become MARKET MAKERS, that is, in addition to buying and selling shares on behalf of private and institutional investors (for which a commission is charged) they can now hold shares on their own account which allows them to buy and sell to make a profit.

stop-loss order An order placed by an investor indicating the amount he/she is prepared to lose on a particular investment. It could be specified as 10% below the purchase price. For example if an investor purchases shares at 100p each with a stop loss order as indicated then if the share price falls to 90p it will signal the order to sell to limit his/her loss. Also a stop loss order can be placed to track the share price. In this case the order to sell would be triggered when the share price falls 10% below its highest value. For example if the shares were to increase to 125p and subsequently fall by 10% to 112.5p the order would be invoked to sell.

straddle The simultaneous buying of a call and a put OPTION in the same UNDERLYING INSTRUMENT (for example, shares, commodities etc) with the same expiry month and the same EXERCISE PRICE.

street name [USA]   The securities of an individual held in the name of a broker or other nominee rather than the name of the individual.

strike price   See exercise price.

subscription price   The price an investor pays for shares in a NEW ISSUE.

subscription terms   The terms under which an investor can subscribe for shares in a NEW ISSUE.

sum assured [UK]   In a life assurance policy (for example, whole life assurance or endowment assurance), the sum assured is the minimum amount payable to the ASSURED or his/her dependants on the death of the LIFE ASSURED.

superannuation [UK]   An OCCUPATIONAL PENSION SCHEME.

support level   The price level at which a security stops falling.

surrender   The encashment of a life policy, for example an ENDOWMENT ASSURANCE policy, by the ASSURED, prior to its MATURITY.

surrender value [USA]   The amount of cash available upon the termination of a CASH VALUE INSURANCE policy. [UK] The cash value of, for example, an ENDOWMENT ASSURANCE policy at any time throughout the TERM prior to its MATURITY. During the early years of the term the surrendering of such policies results in very little return compared with premiums paid. See traded endowment policy. See paid up policy.

swap   The selling of one security and the buying of another in order to realise a higher yield. *currency swap*   An arrangement whereby two parties (for example two companies) agree to exchange responsibilities for the repayment of two different currency loans. For example a UK company may wish to set up a subsidiary in France and would need a loan in French francs. Similarly a French company may wish to take out a loan in pounds sterling. The probability is that the UK company will be able to borrow in pounds sterling at a lower interest rate than in French francs. This would also be the case for the French company that is, it would be able to borrow French francs at a cheaper interest rate than in pounds sterling. The two companies then exchange loan responsibilities and by so doing each obtains a currency loan at a lower interest rate. *interest rate swap*   An arrangement whereby two parties (for example two companies) agree to exchange responsibilities for fixed and variable rates of interest repayments. For example company A may require a fixed interest rate so as to be sure as to what the repayments will be. However company B may prefer a variable rate although it can obtain a fixed rate below that of company A perhaps by 2%. The two companies then exchange loans with, for example, company A taking on the fixed loan and paying 1% to company B. Thus both companies obtain the type of loan each requires at a cheaper rate than that directly available from a bank.

switching   The transferring of assets from one MUTUAL FUND or UNIT TRUST to another within a range of funds with differing objectives such as bonds, capital growth, chemicals, overseas capital growth, all managed by the same mutual fund company or unit trust institution. In the USA, switching can normally be conducted with no charge in a no load range of funds. In a range of load funds a charge is usually incurred. In the UK it is usually the case that one switch per year can be made without cost. Thereafter a charge will be made to the investor.

T

take home pay The amount of money available after all deductions from salary. In the US, the most significant deductions are federal, state and local taxes, pension plan and health insurance. In the UK, the main deductions are income tax, national insurance, pension plan and medical insurance.

tangible assets Physical assets owned by a company or individual which can be seen or touched such as stock, machinery etc. See intangible assets.

taxable earnings See taxable income.

taxable income That part of a person's income which is liable to tax. In the US, this is ADJUSTED GROSS INCOME less allowable DEDUCTIONS. In the UK, taxable income = GROSS INCOME - tax free pay. Tax free pay = ALLOWANCES less deductions.

taxable pay See taxable income.

taxation A levy on persons and companies by a government so as to finance expenditure. In the US, the main taxes are income tax, sales tax and property tax. In the UK, taxation on companies (that is, limited or public limited companies) is known as CORPORATION TAX and is payable on profits. Taxation on individuals may be classified as being direct or indirect as follows:
Direct taxation: INCOME TAX, CAPITAL GAINS TAX, INHERITANCE TAX, COUNCIL TAX and NATIONAL INSURANCE.
Indirect taxation: VALUE ADDED TAX (VAT) and STAMP DUTY.

Taxation Schedules
[USA] Tax forms for listing various income schedules.
Schedule A: Itemized deductions.
Schedule B: Interest and dividend income.
Schedule C: Profit or loss from business.
Schedule D: Capital gains and losses.
Schedule E: Supplemental income and loss.
Schedule SE: Social Security Self Employment tax.

[UK] In the UK income is classified under various headings known as schedules. These are: *Schedule A:* Income from land and property and furnished lettings.

Schedule B: This schedule formerly referred to income from the management of woodlands but is now inoperative.

Schedule C: Interest from government bonds (GILTS) and certain NATIONAL SAVINGS products.

Schedule D:
  Case I: Profits from trade.
  Case II: Profits from professions.
  Case III: Interest from loans and annuities where tax is not deducted at source.
  Case IV: Income from securities held outside the UK.
  Case V: Other income from outside the UK.
  Case VI: Any other income.

Schedule E: Income from employment including bonus payments, BENEFITS IN KIND and pensions. Tax under this schedule is normally collected by way of PAYE.

Schedule F: Dividends paid by companies. This is currently taxed at source.

tax allowances [UK]   These are allowances offset against a person's gross earnings or GROSS INCOME. From these allowances, deductions (for example, BENEFITS IN KIND) are subtracted in order to determine tax free pay. There are basically two types of allowances that is, those of a personal nature which are sums fixed by the government for all individuals who qualify (for example, personal allowance) and those of a non personal nature sometimes known as charges to income or reliefs (for example, premiums paid to a personal pension plan).

tax avoidance   The minimising of tax liability using legal methods in an open manner to the Taxation Authorities. See tax evasion.

tax brackets   The rates of income tax payable on TAXABLE INCOME.

tax codes [UK]   Under the PAYE system of taxing income, tax codes are allocated annually to employees. These codes enable the employer to deduct tax at the correct rate from salaries or wages on a monthly (or weekly) basis for remittance to the INLAND REVENUE. Most codes depict a number followed by a letter. The number refers to the amount of salary payable free of tax (for example if a person's code is 450H, the tax free allowance will be between £4,500 and £4,509 that is, the first three numbers of the net allowances form the number of the code). The letter denotes that various personal and other allowances are included.

tax credit [USA] A specific dollar reduction in tax liability. For example, a taxpayer with a liability of $11,000 and a tax credit of $600 would actually be required to pay $10,400. In the case of a tax deduction the amount in question is deducted from ADJUSTED GROSS INCOME to reduce taxable pay on which tax is then computed. **[UK]** Similarly in the UK, that amount which is deductible from a tax liability. For example, when a company pays a DIVIDEND to its shareholders, tax is first deducted. This deduction is then treated as a tax credit against a person's overall annual tax liability.

tax deductible [USA] An expense which is allowed as a deduction from ADJUSTED GROSS INCOME to reduce TAXABLE INCOME. For example, mortgage interest and state and local taxes.

tax deferred [USA] An investment such as an INDIVIDUAL RETIREMENT ACCOUNT or KEOGH PLAN which is allowed to grow tax free until such time as benefits are taken. Tax is then payable.

tax evasion The minimising of tax liability by failing to declare taxable income or taxable capital gains or by submitting false information to the Taxation Authorities. This is a serious criminal offence with severe consequential penalties. See tax avoidance.

tax exempt [USA] Fee of tax. Most MUNICIPAL BONDS are not subject to federal taxes on the interest.

Tax Exempt Special Savings Account (TESSA) [UK] A five year tax free savings scheme for persons aged 18 and over, introduced by the government in January 1991 and operated by banks and building societies. The maximum amount which can be paid into such schemes over the five year period is £9,000 according to the following schedule: 1st year, £3,000. 2nd year, £1,800. 3rd year, £1,800. 4th year, £1,800. 5th year £600. After five years the interest and capital can be withdrawn free of tax. TESSAs were discontinued on 5th April 1999 although those taken out before this date are allowed to run their full five year term.

tax exile A wealthy person who lives outside his/her own country in order to minimise taxes. Such countries which operate a low rate of tax are known as TAX HAVENS.

tax free pay [UK] A person's ALLOWANCES less DEDUCTIONS.

tax haven A country where companies or individuals may legally take advantage of lower taxation levels.

tax liability   A legal obligation to Taxation Authorities for taxes owed.

tax rate bands   The rates of income tax payable on TAXABLE INCOME.

tax relief   The deduction of certain types of expenditure from gross salary or company profits to limit tax payable. For example pension contributions up to a certain level may be deducted from gross income to reduce taxable pay.

tax return   A form on which certain taxpayers annually list their salary (including pensions), or income from self employment together with benefits in kind, other income and capital gains. This information is used by the Taxation Authorities to assess tax liability.

tax voucher   A paper advice slip issued by companies when paying DIVIDENDS to its shareholders. The voucher indicates a number of items including the date, the dividend rate in pence per share, whether the dividend is interim or final, the number of shares held by the shareholder, the net dividend payable and the TAX CREDIT.

tax year [UK]   The twelve month period commencing 6th April and ending 5th April the following year.

technical analysis   The study of the prices of securities, commodities and currencies etc using past history and charts (see chartist) in order to assess both value-for-money and future trends.

telegraphic transfer   A method of transferring money abroad from one bank to another by telegraphy.

temporary annuity   See annuity.

tenancy agreement   An agreement whereby land/property is leased.

tenancy at will   The occupancy of property by a tenant for an unspecified period. The tenancy can be terminated by either the landlord or tenant at any time.

tenancy in common   A situation where two or more persons own land/property. In the event of the death of one of the owners, his/her interest passes to his/her estate and not the other tenants.

tenant   A person who occupies land/property on a LEASE basis.

tender **1.** A written quotation submitted by a person or company in competition with others in order to attempt to win a contract. Usually (but not always), the company with the lowest tender is awarded the contract. **2.** In share dealing an offer by tender relates to potential buyers specifying the price at which they are prepared to purchase, the highest bidder being awarded the shares. In some cases buyers are asked to bid above a minimum price.

tender offer See tender 2.

term A specified period of time (that is, the term). See term life insurance / term assurance.

term life insurance [USA] term assurance [UK] A LIFE INSURANCE policy in which cover is provided for a specified period of time (the term). The death benefit (UK SUM ASSURED) is paid if the death of the INSURED (UK LIFE ASSURED) occurs during the term. If the insured survives the term, the contract ceases and no benefit is payable.

terminal bonus [UK] An additional bonus paid to reflect the overall performance of a WITH PROFITS life assurance policy at MATURITY or prior death of the LIFE ASSURED. See reversionary bonus.

testament A WILL.

testate The situation which exists when a person dies having made a will. See intestate.

testator A person who makes a WILL.

testatrix The feminine form of TESTATOR.

thin market A market in which unusually few transactions occur. This may apply to the shares of a specific company or the market as a whole.

third market The trading of exchange listed securities in the OVER THE COUNTER market.

third party The person who claims against an insured person when loss or damage to property or injury has occurred as a result of the insured person's negligence. See third party insurance.

third party fire and theft See motor insurance.

third party insurance   The insurance of a person's legal liability (that is, a contract between an INSURER and the INSURED person) to cover against causing injury to another person or persons (the THIRD PARTY) or loss or damage to their property. An example in the UK is third party MOTOR INSURANCE. In the event of the insured causing damage to a third party's vehicle, his/her insurers would be liable to reimburse the third party. However the insured would not be able to claim for damages to his/her vehicle. COMPREHENSIVE INSURANCE would be required for this.

thrift institution [USA]   A depository organisation for savings including SAVINGS AND LOAN ASSOCIATIONS and MUTUAL SAVINGS BANKS. Deposits are in the main used for home mortgage loans.

tick   **1.** An upward or downward movement in the price of a security. **2.** The minimum price fluctuation of a FUTURES or OPTIONS CONTRACT.

ticker tape [USA]   The machine which displays stock symbols, prices and volumes and transmits world wide.

tied agent   See company representative.

time deposit [USA]   A SAVINGS ACCOUNT or CERTIFICATE OF DEPOSIT whose funds are subject to notice (such as 30 days) prior to withdrawal. In the event of early withdrawal a penalty will normally be incurred.

time to expiry   The time remaining before a WARRANT is due to expire. After the expiry date a warrant has no value.

time value   **1.** The amount by which an option's PREMIUM(4) exceeds its INTRINSIC VALUE(1). Time value reflects the remaining life of an OPTION. **2.** The value attached to a WARRANT by virtue of its TIME TO EXPIRY. For example, a warrant which can be exercised during the month of September for any of the forthcoming five years would have a greater time value than if its expiry date was one year hence.

title   The right to legal ownership of PROPERTY.

top slicing [UK]   A method of assessing the INCOME TAX liability on the proceeds of LIFE ASSURANCE policies. Although income tax is not normally payable on benefits from QUALIFYING POLICIES, liabilities may exist if the policy is cashed in early, that is, within ten years (or within 75% of the policy term if this happens to be shorter) or if it becomes a PAID UP POLICY. The proceeds of NON QUALIFYING LIFE POLICIES are liable to income tax. Assessment of income tax is on the CHARGEABLE GAIN (which is the amount of the policy proceeds less total PREMIUMS (1) paid) if a CHARGEABLE EVENT occurs.

total return The movement in price of a security where the dividends are reinvested.

tracker fund A fund which invests to perform in line with a stock exchange index such as the STANDARD AND POOR'S 500 COMPOSITE INDEX or the FT-A ALL SHARE INDEX. The performance of such a fund will accordingly 'track' the index in question. Also known as an index fund.

traded options OPTIONS on shares, currencies, commodities which are themselves traded on an exchange.

trade reference A reference given by one company to another regarding the creditworthiness of another company whom it supplies with goods. It is usual for two or more trade references together with a bank reference to be requested by companies prior to supplying goods or services on credit.

Tradepoint Investment Exchange A London based exchange which opened on 21st September 1995 currently dealing in over 900 of the most actively traded UK equities. Tradepoint is an electronic order driven market accessible via a standard IBM PC where brokers, market makers and investing institutions participate on an anonymous basis and enter buy or sell orders. For the most liquid stocks, trades are completed the moment a corresponding buy or sell order is entered by another participant. Less liquid stocks are traded by way of computer matching following the accumulation of orders after periods of time. Trades are guaranteed by the LONDON CLEARING HOUSE (LCH) and settlement is via CREST. Tradepoint is a RECOGNISED INVESTMENT EXCHANGE (RIE) and is regulated by the FINANCIAL SERVICES AUTHORITY (FSA).

trading unit [USA] The minimum number of shares, bonds or commodities which are traded in a transaction on an exchange. This number is usually 100 for shares.

traditional options OPTIONS on shares which, unlike TRADED OPTIONS, are not transferable and must be exercised on specific dates. In order to make a profit, the owner of the options has to purchase them (assuming the option price is attractive on the relevant date) and then sell them on the market.

tranche [USA] One of a combined group of related securities which offer various risk, reward and maturity alternatives. **[UK]** A portion or slice. The term could be typically used to describe part of a PRIVATISATION which is being offered in stages.

transfer The change of ownership of property.

transfer agent [USA] An agent such as a bank which acts for a corporation in relation to the maintaining of records of stock and bond owners and other associated matters such as lost certificates.

transfer payments [USA] A transfer of money from the government to individuals, typically Social Security, disability payments and unemployment benefits.

transfer tax [USA] A federal tax imposed on the purchase of securities. Similar to stamp duty in the UK.

transfer value [UK] The value of a PENSION fund which would be available for transfer into an alternative type of plan either with the same or an alternative pension provider.

travel insurance Insurance which gives cover to persons travelling usually to foreign countries on holidays or business travel. Some of the benefits include reimbursement for medical expenses, loss of luggage and money, cancellation or curtailment, departure delay and loss of passport etc. Lump sums are payable for personal accident covering death, loss of limbs or eyes or permanent disablement. Certain legal expenses for claims against a third party causing injury to the INSURED are also payable plus personal liability cover if the insured causes injury to a third party or their property. The maximum amounts of cover for all the above cases are stipulated by the insurers.

traveler's checks [USA] traveller's cheques [UK] Checks issued by CREDIT CARD and CHARGE CARD companies and banks etc which enable the holder to obtain cash or pay for goods and services when visiting a foreign country. The checks are signed by the traveler on their receipt and again when payment is being made. They are covered against loss provided the issuing company is notified within a specified period.

Treasury Bill [UK] A government security usually with a life of three months but also up to one year maturity. Such bills are issued by the government at a discount and redeemable at PAR with no interest payable. They provide a principle way of financing borrowing. Other methods of

---

government borrowing include the issuing of GILT EDGED STOCKS (gilts) usually fixed interest, with a variety of REDEMPTION DATES.

Treasury securities (treasuries) [USA]   Debt obligations issued by the US government and secured by FULL FAITH AND CREDIT. Income from treasuries is subject to federal tax but not state and local taxes. They fall into three categories, Treasury bills, Treasury bonds and Treasury notes.

> *Treasury bills (T-bills):* Short term securities with minimum denominations of $10,000 and maturities of three months, six months and one year. They are issued at a discount to FACE VALUE.

> *Treasury bonds:* Long term securities with minimum denominations of $1,000 and maturities of ten years or more.

> *Treasury notes:* Medium term securities with minimum denominations from $1,000 and maturities of one to ten years.

trust   An arrangement which empowers one or more persons (the TRUSTEES) to safeguard the assets such as property and money of another person or persons (the BENEFICIARIES).

trust deed   The legal document which sets out the terms of a TRUST. Included will be the names of the TRUSTEES and BENEFICIARIES and details of the trust property/monies.

trustee   A person appointed to manage and safeguard the assets of a TRUST.

turnover [USA]   The volume of trading in shares expressed as a percentage of total shares listed on an exchange for a specific period, for example, a day. **[UK]** A company's total sales figure for a given trading period such as annual turnover.

U

uberrimae fidei   See utmost good faith.

umbrella personal liability insurance [USA]   LIABILITY INSURANCE giving excess cover over and above that cover provided by other policies. For example if general policies give total liability insurance cover of $400,000, an umbrella policy could typically provide cover of $1 million. If a claim of $700,000 were made the umbrella policy would pay out only after the $400,000 has been first exhausted.

uncovered   See naked.

undated stocks   Fixed interest stocks which have no REDEMPTION DATE.

underlying instrument   The instrument, such as shares and commodities on which a FUTURES or OPTIONS CONTRACT is based.

underwriter   1.   A financial institution which, in return for a fee or commission (underwriting commission) agrees to purchase unsold shares in a NEW ISSUE. **2.**   A person or company who assesses risk with regard to an item to be insured and if acceptable accordingly calculates the premium payable.

underwriting commission   See underwriter 1.

unearned income   Income received from sources such as dividends from shares and bonds, that is, income which has not been earned by working.

unemployment benefit [USA]   Benefit received from a state Department of Labor when a previously employed person becomes unemployed. That person must be able to verify previous employment and that he/she is actively seeking new employment.   Benefits usually expire after 26 weeks.   **[UK]**   Benefit received from the Benefit Office when a previously employed person becomes unemployed.   These payments are liable to income tax.

unfranked income   Income received on which tax has not been paid.

unfunded pension plan [USA]   A pension plan which is funded by an employer from current income for the benefit of retirees.

unified tax credit [USA]   A federal tax credit which may be deducted from estate tax and gift tax liability.

uninsured motorist insurance [USA]   Automobile insurance which gives cover to the insured and passengers in the event of vehicle damage and personal injury caused by an uninsured motorist.

unissued stock [USA]   A corporation's AUTHORIZED STOCK which is as yet unissued.

unit linked   See unit linked policy.

unit linked endowment assurance   See endowment assurance.

unit linked life assurance   See unit linked policy.

unit linked policy [UK]   1. A LIFE ASSURANCE policy in which a portion of the PREMIUM(1) is used to purchase life cover (the SUM ASSURED) with the balance invested in an authorised UNIT TRUST/trusts. The return on the policy is thus linked to the performance of the units in the unit trust. Unit linked policies include single premium bonds or INVESTMENT BONDS, unit linked endowment assurance and unit linked whole life assurance. See endowment assurance. See whole life assurance. **2.** A PENSION plan in which members' contributions are used to purchase units in an AUTHORISED UNIT TRUST.

unit linked whole of life assurance   See whole life assurance.

unit of trading [USA]   The minimum number of shares, bonds or commodities which are traded in a transaction on an exchange. This number is usually 100 for shares.

unit trust [UK]   A collective investment scheme which enables small private investors to partake in ownership of a diversified portfolio of shares. It is known as an OPEN END fund since there is no fixed amount of CAPITAL in the trust. Management is by way of professional fund managers who invest in securities to achieve the trust's objectives such as capital growth, income or a combination of both. The TRUSTEES, typically a bank, ensure the managers operate the trust in accordance with the TRUST DEED. Each investor is allocated units in the trust which represent the amount of his/her investment at the time of purchase. The price at which units are sold to investors is known as the offer price or buying price. When such units are ultimately sold by the investor the price obtained is known as the bid price or selling price. The difference between the offer and bid prices is known as the BID/OFFER spread. Bid and offer prices of authorised and other unit trusts are published daily in leading newspapers such as the Financial Times, which enable the investor to regularly check on the value of his/her units.

unitisation The conversion of an INVESTMENT TRUST into UNIT TRUST.

unitised with profits [UK] WITH PROFITS and investment linked funds combined in the same contract with the choice of SWITCHING between them.

cash value life insurance [USA] A LIFE INSURANCE policy which pays a benefit on the death of the INSURED but which also provides a savings element where benefits are payable before death.

universal life insurance [USA] A combination of TERM LIFE INSURANCE and a savings element which is invested to provide a cash value build up. The policy is flexible in that the death benefit, savings element and premiums can be reviewed and altered from time to time as a policyholder's circumstances change.

unlisted securities [USA] Securities which are not traded on a main exchange such as the NEW YORK STOCK EXCHANGE. Instead they are traded in the OVER THE COUNTER market. **[UK]** Shares (usually in small companies) which are not listed on a RECOGNISED INVESTMENT EXCHANGE. A limited number of unlisted securities have traded since 1980 on the UNLISTED SECURITIES MARKET (USM) which however closed at the end of 1996. The USM was replaced by the ALTERNATIVE INVESTMENT MARKET (AIM).

unlisted securities market A market set up by the LONDON STOCK EXCHANGE in 1980 for the trading of shares of small to medium sized companies which did not qualify for a full LISTING. The USM was discontinued at the end of 1996. See alternative investment market (AIM).

unpaid dividend A dividend which has been declared by a corporation but as yet unpaid.

unsecured loan A loan where the lender has no entitlement to any of the borrower's assets in the event of the borrower failing to make the loan repayments. Such a loan normally carries a higher interest rate than a SECURED LOAN.

unsecured loan stock   LOAN STOCK issued by a company but without security, that is, the holder of the loan stock does not have entitlement to any of the company's assets in the event of non repayment of the loan.

upper earnings level [UK]   The earnings level of an employee above which no further Class 1 NATIONAL INSURANCE CONTRIBUTIONS are payable.

U S Federal Reserve   See Federal Reserve.

utilities   Companies which provide essential services such as electricity, gas and water etc.

utmost good faith   All contracts of insurance are subject to utmost good faith in that persons are obliged to disclose any detail which may be of importance to the insurers whether or not it is requested.

V

valuation   The VALUE or worth of a PORTFOLIO of investments recorded on a statement.

value   The worth or desirability of something expressed as an amount of money.

value added tax (VAT) [UK]   An indirect tax levied on goods and services in the UK. A company or trader registered for VAT pays suppliers VAT additionally to the cost of goods or services purchased which is known as INPUT TAX. Also VAT is added to the sales cost of their product when invoicing customers which is known as OUTPUT TAX. The difference between output tax and input tax is payable to the government department, HER MAJESTY'S CUSTOMS AND EXCISE.

valued policy   An insurance policy in which the value of the insured item is defined and agreed at the commencement of the policy. In the event of a total loss the agreed amount is paid by the insurer without the need for further proof of value.

variable annuity   See annuity.

variable interest rate   Interest rates offered by banks and financial institutions on loans or deposits which are liable to change according to circumstances. For example a movement in the interest rate set by the government would usually be an influence.

variable life insurance [USA]   A form of CASH VALUE LIFE INSURANCE in which the cash value of the policy may be invested in shares and bonds etc. according to the insured's choice.

variable rate certificate   A CERTIFICATE OF DEPOSIT whose interest rate varies and is dependent on an influence such as PRIME RATE.

variable rate mortgage (VRM)   A MORTGAGE where the interest rate is not fixed and which is dependent on influences such as interest rates on TREASURY SECURITIES in the US or BASE RATE in the UK.

variance   The difference between budgeted and actual costs.

variation margin Profits and losses on open FUTURES CONTRACTS, which are revalued daily at the SETTLEMENT PRICE, which are subsequently paid to or received from the CLEARING HOUSE.

vendor A person or company selling goods and property.

venture capital Capital invested into small and young companies in return for equity ownership. Such companies, often manufacturing high technology products, have potential for significant growth but at much higher risk.

venture capital trust [UK] A company similar to an INVESTMENT TRUST in which the majority of its capital is invested in small unquoted companies (companies whose shares are not quoted on a RECOGNISED INVESTMENT EXCHANGE). There is a limit on how much may be invested in a single company and a limit on the capital value of companies in which the trust may invest funds. Since this type of trust invests in a range of companies the risk involved with VENTURE CAPITAL tends to be spread.

vesting Conversion. For example the vesting of a pension fund is its conversion into a pension.

Visa An international card scheme providing a range of payment services.

volatility The significant price variations of a security, commodity or market as a whole over a short period of time. Large fluctuations reflect high volatility.

volume A reference to the amount of shares traded on a stock exchange for a given period.

voluntary deductible employee contribution plan [USA] A type of pension plan in which an employee elects to have regular payments deducted from each paycheck.

voluntary liquidation [USA] The liquidation of a company approved by its shareholders. **[UK]** *1. Members' voluntary liquidation or winding up:* The winding up of a company voluntarily with the directors' declaration that debts are payable. *2. Creditors' voluntary liquidation or winding up:* The winding up of a company with a resolution stating the company is unable to trade due to its debts.

voting right   The entitlement of the owner of COMMON STOCK or ORDINARY SHARES to vote in person or by PROXY at ANNUAL MEETINGS or ANNUAL GENERAL MEETINGS.

voting stock [USA]   Stock, typically COMMON STOCK, which confers on the owner the right to vote on election of directors and other corporate matters.

voucher   A receipt for the payment of money confirming an entry in book keeping.

W

waiting period [USA]   The period, prior to payments by the insurers to a policyholder of DISABILITY INCOME INSURANCE after a claim, during which no payments are made. This is typically several months. Also known as elimination period. Known as deferment period in the UK.

waiver of premium   An arrangement in LIFE INSURANCE, which, in return for some increase in premium, ensures that policyholders have their premiums paid during periods of absence from work due to illness or accident. There is usually an elimination period (or waiting period), UK DEFERMENT PERIOD, typically several months, after which the insurers commence payments.

warrant [USA]   See stock warrants. **[UK]** A transferable security which grants the owner the right but not the obligation to purchase shares in a company at a specific price (EXERCISE PRICE) at a future date/dates, or during a future period/periods. They do not pay dividends nor do they carry voting rights. They are traded on stock exchanges. Warrants offer gearing (share price/warrant price) which results in a magnified up or down percentage movement of the warrant price following a change in share price. Most warrants are issued by INVESTMENT TRUSTS. See PREMIUM. See TIME VALUE. See INTRINSIC VALUE.

warranty   A contract in which a seller commits to a buyer that any faulty workmanship or product failure occurring within a specified period will be rectified at no cost to the buyer. Typical products covered by warranty include appliances, automobiles and machinery.

weak market   A stock market where volume is low and the spread is high.

wedding insurance   Insurance to give protection against financial loss in relation to a wedding. Items typically covered include costs arising out of unavoidable cancellation (such as the venue being unable to hold the ceremony, wedding transport failing to arrive), damage to hired dress wear such as bridal gown, bridesmaids' dresses and morning suits, loss/ damage to or retaking of photographs and loss of or damage to wedding presents and wedding rings etc. There is a specified maximum amount which can be claimed under each section and a DEDUCTIBLE amount also applies.

white knight   A company (or person) making a welcome takeover bid usually with an improved offer for another company which has been the subject of an unwanted hostile bid from another party known as a BLACK KNIGHT. See also grey knight.

whole life insurance [USA]   A life insurance policy, with level premiums, which provides a stated benefit on the death of the life insured and a savings element which accumulates a cash value. The cash value dividends or interest are allowed to build up tax deferred. The insured is able to redeem the cash value or borrow against it which is known as a policy loan. Any part of a loan which is unpaid at the death of the insured is deducted from the face value. **whole life assurance [UK]**   A LIFE ASSURANCE policy which pays out a sum of money (the SUM ASSURED) on the death of the LIFE ASSURED. If a whole life policy is encashed in its early years any proceeds returnable to the policyholder will normally be below the value of the premiums paid up to cancellation.

will   A document which sets out how a person wishes his/her estate or property to be dispersed after his/her death. The document must be signed by the testator/testatrix (the person making the will) in the presence of two witnesses who must also sign. An executor (female form executrix) or executors are appointed by the testator to ensure that his/her wishes are carried out.

windfall shares [UK]   The shares of privatised UTILITIES companies such as National Power and BG.

windfall tax [UK]   A one off tax imposed by the government in the budget of July 1997 on the profits of privatised UTILITIES companies. It was applied to fund the government's Welfare to Work programme which was instigated to assist provide employment and to help lone parents and the disabled for the period up to 2002. The profits were assessed as the difference between a company's privatised sale price and its average value over the subsequent four years. The tax was levied on a number of companies including BAA, BG, British Telecom, British Energy, Centrica, National Power, PowerGen, the regional electricity companies and the water and sewerage companies and payable in two instalments on or before 1st December 1997 and 1st December 1998.

winding up   See liquidation.

withholding [USA]   A deduction from an employee's salary by an employer for federal, state and local tax liabilities.

with profits [UK]   An expression referring to a LIFE ASSURANCE or PENSION policy which participates in receiving part of the life company's profits which derive from investments in equities, property and fixed interest securities etc. They are paid by way of REVERSIONARY BONUSES and TERMINAL BONUSES. This principle is applied to WITH PROFITS BONDS, with profits endowment assurance, with profits whole life assurance, low cost endowment assurance, low cost whole life assurance and low start (escalating) endowment assurance. Also with profits pension plans. See endowment assurance. See whole life assurance.

with profits bond   A BOND, purchased with a lump sum, affiliated to WITH PROFITS growth and more suitable for long term investment.

without prejudice   Basic meaning is without loss of any rights. It is a term used in offers intended to guard against any inference of waiver of rights and in correspondence seeking to negotiate a compromise, in which case the communication so made cannot be used in evidence in court proceedings.

working capital   A company's current assets (cash, debtors, work in progress) less its current liabilities (creditors, taxes due). This capital is used by a company to run its business.

writ   A written order issued by a court instructing the defendant to appear in court to answer charges made by the plaintiff.

writer   A person who makes an OPENING SALE of an OPTION contract. Upon notification of EXERCISE by the option HOLDER (the buyer), the writer is obliged to deliver or take delivery of the UNDERLYING INSTRUMENT (for example, shares, commodities etc).

X

xa [UK]   Another way of writing ex all. This means that shares bought in a company are without entitlement to current DIVIDENDS, RIGHTS ISSUES or SCRIP ISSUES. Such entitlement remains with the seller of the shares.

xc   Another way of writing ex scrip or ex capitalisation. Shares bought in a company are without entitlement to current SCRIP ISSUES. Such entitlement remains with the seller of the shares.

xd   Another way of writing ex dividend. Shares bought in a company are without entitlement to current DIVIDENDS. Such entitlement remains with the seller of the shares.

xr   Another way of writing ex rights. Shares bought in a company are without entitlement to current RIGHTS ISSUES. Such entitlement remains with the seller of the shares.

xw [USA]   Another way of writing ex warrants. Shares bought in a company are without entitlement to warrants.

Y

Yankee A dollar denominated bond issued in the USA by a foreign bank..

year end dividend An additional dividend paid at the end of the trading year and based on company profits.

yearling [UK] A local authority bond normally issued for one year.

yield The annual income received from an asset expressed as a percentage of its cost. If the asset is a bank account, the income received is known as interest. For shares the income is known as the DIVIDEND. In the case of debt securities or fixed interest securities such as BONDS, the income is known as the COUPON. Yield may be indicated in a number of ways:

dividend yield: The annual income received from shares in a company divided by its current share price.

nominal yield: The annual income from a fixed interest security that is, the coupon, divided by its nominal or PAR VALUE.

current yield (earnings yield, flat yield, running yield): The annual income from a fixed interest security divided by its current market price.

yield to maturity / redemption yield: An indication of the overall return of a fixed interest security if held to REDEMPTION. It takes into account both the current yield and the capital gain or loss divided by the number of years remaining to redemption (maturity).

yield curve A curve which plots current yields of fixed interest securities against their times to redemption (maturity). This enables investors to compare the yields of short, medium and long term securities at a given time.

yield gap [UK] A comparison between the average yield from shares (dividend yield) and the average current yield from long dated GILTS (15 years or more to redemption).

yuppie A word which became popular in the 1980s meaning young upwardly mobile professional.

Z

zero coupon bond [USA]   A bond where no interest is paid during its life. Such a bond is purchased at a substantial discount and the accumulated interest is added to the face value at maturity. Although not paid, the annual interest is taxable as income.   **[UK]**   A bond which pays no interest throughout its life and which pays a capital gain by being issued at a substantial discount to the maturity value. Thus there may be a liability to CAPITAL GAINS TAX. Depending on circumstances this may offer an advantage to certain taxpayers since there is no income tax liability.

zero dividend preference shares (zeros) [UK]   PREFERENCE SHARES which receive no dividends throughout their lives. Instead a fixed known amount is paid at maturity.

zero rated [UK]   A term relating to VALUE ADDED TAX (VAT). It refers to goods (for example, food and books) which are taxable but at a zero rate. The significance of this rating is that businesses selling such goods may claim back their INPUT TAX (the VAT which they have paid to their suppliers). Businesses which provide goods and services which are VAT exempt (for example, stamps and postal services) are not able to reclaim input tax.

Acronyms

A

ADR	American depositary receipt
AGM	annual general meeting
AIM	Alternative Investment Market
AITC	Association of Investment Trust Companies
AMEX	American Stock Exchange
AMT	alternative minimum tax
APCIMS	Association of Private Client Investment Managers and Stockbrokers
APR	annual percentage rate
ARM	adjustable rate mortgage
ARPS	adjustable rate preferred stock
ATM	automated teller machine
AUTIF	Association of Unit Trusts and Investment Funds
AVC	additional voluntary contributions

B

BAN	bond anticipation note
BE	bill of exchange
BOP	balance of payments
BOT	balance of trade

C

CBI	Confederation of British Industry
CGT	capital gains tax
CPI	consumer price index

E

EC	European Community
EEC	European Economic Community
EFTA	European Free Trade Association
EFTS	electronic funds transfer system
EMS	European Monetary System
EPS	earnings per share
ERISA	Employee Retirement Income Security Act
ERM	Exchange Rate Mechanism
ERNIE	Electronic Random Number Indicator Equipment
ESOP	employee stock ownership plan

F

FDIC	Federal Deposit Insurance Corporation
FICA	Federal Insurance Contributions Act
FNMA	Federal National Mortgage Association (Fannie Mae)
FSA	Financial Services Authority
FSAVC	free standing additional voluntary contributions

G

GATT	General Agreement on Tariffs and Trade
GDP	gross domestic product
GEMMs	Gilt Edged Market Makers
GNMA	Government National Mortgage Association (Ginnie Mae)
GNP	gross national product
GPM	graduated payment mortgage
G7	Group of Seven

I

ICS	Investors Compensation Scheme
IFA	independent financial adviser
IFP	Institute of Financial Planning
IMRO	Investment Management Regulatory Organisation
IPE	International Petroleum Exchange
IPO	initial public offering
IRA	individual retirement account
IRS	Internal Revenue Service
ISA	individual savings account

L

LBO	leveraged buyout
LBMA	London Bullion Market Association
LCH	London Clearing House
LCE	London Commodity Exchange
LIBOR	London Inter Bank Offered Rate
LIFFE	London International Financial Futures and Options Exchange
LME	London Metal Exchange

M

MIB	Motor Insurers' Bureau
MIRAS	mortgage interest relief at source

N

NAIC	National Association of Investors Corporation
NASD	National Association of Securities Dealers
NAV	net asset value
NI	National Insurance
NMS	normal market size
NPV	no par value
NYM	New York Mercantile Exchange
NYSE	New York Stock Exchange

O

OEIC	open ended investment company
OPAS	Occupational Pensions Advisory Service
OPRA	Occupational Pensions Regulatory Authority
OTC	over the counter
OTS	Office of Thrift Supervision

P

P&L	profit and loss statement
PAYE	pay as you earn
PBGC	Pension Benefit Guaranty Corporation
PEP	personal equity plan
P/E Ratio	price earnings ratio
PET	potentially exempt transfer
PIA	Personal Investment Authority
PIBS	permanent interest bearing shares
PIN	personal identification number
PLC	public limited company
PSNCR	Public Sector Net Cash Requirement

R

RAM	reverse annuity mortgage
REIT	real estate investment trust
RPI	retail price index

S

SAM	shared appreciation mortgage
SAYE	save as you earn
SEAQ	Stock Exchange Automated Quotation system
SEC	Securities and Exchange Commission
SEP	Simplified Employee Pension Plan
SEPON	Stock Exchange Pool Nominee

SERPS	State Earnings Related Pension Scheme
SFA	Securities and Futures Authority
SIB	Securities and Investments Board
SIPC	Securities Investor Protection Corporation
SRO	Self Regulating Organisation

T

TESSA	Tax Exempt Special Savings Account

U

UK	United Kingdom
USA	United States of America

V

VAT	value added tax
VRM	variable rate mortgage

X

xa	ex all
xc	ex scrip or ex capitalisation
xd	ex dividend
xr	ex rights
xw	ex warrants

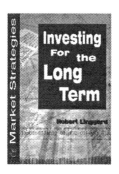

Understand Shares in a Day

Shows how the share market really works. Inexperienced investors will learn: ❏ About different types of shares ... ❏ Why share prices fluctuate... ❏ How to read the financial pages ... ❏ How shares are bought and sold ... ❏ How risk can be spread with investment and unit trusts ... ❏ How to build a portfolio of shares ...❏ The risks and rewards associated with Penny Shares

Once this basic groundwork has been covered, the book explores more complex ideas which will appeal to both beginners and more experienced investors alike, including: ● How to value shares ● How equity options are used by professional investors to 'gear' profits and hedge against falling share prices.

£6.95/$11.95

Understand Derivatives in a Day

Financial derivatives are used as highly-geared vehicles for making money, saving money or preventing its loss. They also have the ability to exploit volatility, guarantee results and avoid taxes. But only if they are used correctly.

Learn...How private investors get started... To Hedge, Straddle and control Risk... Ways to limit the downside but not the upside... About risk free derivative strategies... Trading Psychology - Fear, Hope and Greed... Also, the History of Derivatives; Currency Speculation; Long and Short puts; Tarantula Trading; and much more. £6.95/$11.95

Understand Bonds & Gilts in a Day

This handy title shows potential investors, and those with an interest in the bond markets, how to assess the potential risks and rewards, giving a simple to follow set of criteria on which to base investment decisions. Having shown the inexperienced investor how to go about buying bonds, it also teaches even the most arithmetically shy how to calculate the yield on a bond and plan an income based portfolio. The confusing terminology used in the bond market is clearly explained with working definitions of many terms and a comprehensive glossary.

£6.95/$11.95

Investing on the Internet

The world of investment is a dangerous place. No matter how independent your financial advisor claims to be, they always seem to sell you a 'product' with the highest commission to them; witness the pensions scandal of the 80s and early 90s. Even if you receive good advice, there is a huge slab of commission to be paid.

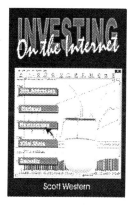

That is why many investors are turning to the Internet. There, they are able to research companies in depth, examine price movements, discuss the merits with other investors and finally invest their money with very service low charges (due to the automation of the process).

Finding exactly what you want on the Internet is extremely difficult. There are several hundred million sites already in existence, and an estimated six million new pages are being added every week. Unfortunately there is no central repository for information and no catalogue of web sites. As a result, searching for the pages you want to view is a time consuming task, and frustrating when irrelevant pages and bad hits get in your way.

INVESTING on the Internet provides a detailed listing of the best sites in this category. Each site is reviewed in terms of content, layout and design, as well as the technical aspects such as speed of downloading, size of graphics and ease of internal navigation.

£4.95/$9.95

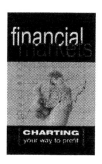

Timing The Financial Markets: Charting Your Way to Profit

Timing The Financial Markets shows all levels of investors, step-by-step, how to construct charts and graphs of price movements for bonds, shares and commodities. Then it explains, in easy-to-understand language, how to interpret the results and turn them into profit.   £6.95/$11.95

Book Ordering

Please complete the form below or use a plain piece of paper and send to:

Europe/Asia
TTL, PO Box 200, Harrogate HG1 2YR, England (or fax to 01423-526035, or email: sales@net-works.co.uk).

USA/Canada
Trafalgar Square, PO Box 257, Howe Hill Road, North Pomfret, Vermont 05053 (or fax to 802-457-1913, call toll free 800-423-4525, or email: tsquare@sover.net)

Postage and handling charge:
UK - £1 for first book, and 50p for each additional book
USA - $5 for first book, and $2 for each additional book (all shipments by UPS, please provide street address).
Elsewhere - £3 for first book, and £1.50 for each additional book via surface post (for airmail and courier rates, please fax or email for a price quote)

Book	Qty	Price

❏ I enclose payment for _____

Postage

Total:

❏ Please debit my Visa/Amex/Mastercard No:

Expiry date: [ ][ ][ ][ ]   Signature:

Name: _____

Address: _____

_____

_____

Postcode/Zip: _____

dictpf